Step-by-Step Guide
for
Dealing with Unfair and Illegal
Debt Collection Tactics

You Really Can Fight Back!

Richard Rafferty

January 2005:	Original Version
April 2005:	1st Revision
October 2005:	2nd Revision
September 2007:	3rd Revision
January 2009:	4th Revision

ISBN: 978-1-4269-0571-1 (sc)

ISBN: 978-1-4269- 0573-5 (e-book)

Book Cover by Kyara Rafferty

Acknowledgments

Thanks to my loving wife who has stood beside me, for better or worse, for over 25 years and supported me through the good times and the bad. Without her love and support, my ability to help others would cease to exist. I owe her a debt of gratitude that can never be paid.

Contents

Why this Book?

In 1998 I designed a web site called Fair Debt Collection as a way to reach out to people who needed information for dealing with unfair and illegal debt collection tactics but could not afford to pay attorney consultation fees. I noticed there was (and still is) a lot of misinformation floating around the Internet about what debt collectors and creditors can and cannot do when attempting to collect debts. Although the Fair Debt Collection Practices Act (FDCPA) has been in effect for many years, there are still too many consumers who are unaware of the FDCPA or how it protects consumers from unethical collection practices.

In the beginning, the site was not much more than a copy of the FDCPA and a few frequently asked questions (FAQ) about consumers' rights under this federal law. I immediately started receiving questions via email, phone calls, even snail mail from people who were being harassed by debt collectors.

First of all, I am not an attorney so I cannot give legal advice but even after informing people of that fact, they didn't care, they were being harassed by debt collectors and wanted to know how to make the harassment stop. After a few months, the calls became overwhelming so I had to remove my phone number from the site. Instead I offered to answer questions via email and included a warning on the site that I would answer general questions but would refer them to consumer attorneys in their area for legal questions.

By the end of 1999, I was answering hundreds of questions a week and by 2002 that ballooned to over one thousand questions per week. As questions rolled in, I added them to my Frequently Asked Questions page. Many people were asking the same or very similar questions so I added additional pages to the site to answer questions about specific subjects. Eventually the site grew to well over 100 pages and climbed to the top of the search engines where it still remains to this day.

From the beginning, the web site offered free information to clear up myths about debt collection and over the years, it grew into a resource that consumers, creditors, lenders, and even debt collectors use. Based on the first web site, I designed several other web sites, all free and dedicated to helping people deal with issues such as credit repair, student loans in default, small claims courts, bankruptcy, child support collection, credit cards, and bank foreclosures.

Over the years, I've had credit counselors, consumers and even attorneys ask me to put my information into a book that can be used as a desk-top reference. As a full-time educator, finding the time to put together a book was difficult. But, eventually I pieced together the original version of this book. I called it an eGuide and offered it as a free download on my web site. Afterwards, I built and launched several more debt and credit web sites to help people but the cost of maintaining them became too expensive. So, I started selling the eGuide online to help pay for web site hosting and maintenance fees. Doing so allowed me to continue offering my websites as free information resources.

Of course, whenever one provides information, especially free information about consumer rights and consumer laws it must be made clear that information is not the same as legal advice. So, to be absolutely clear, here is my legal disclaimer…

Legal Notice

I am not an attorney and therefore cannot provide legal advice or services. As such, the information presented here is for educational purposes and should not be used as a substitute for professional legal counsel or other competent advice. The information in this document is protected by one or more worldwide copyright treaties and may not be reprinted, copied, redistributed, transmitted, hosted, displayed, or stored electronically or by any means whatsoever, without express written permission of Rich's Enterprises, LLC. All names of people, trademarks, service marks, company names, and brand names are property of their respective owners and are used in editorial commentary as permitted under constitutional law. While every attempt has been made to ensure information contained in this guide has been obtained from reliable sources, the author and publisher are not responsible for any errors or omissions and disclaim any liability for personal loss caused by the use of, misuse of or inability to use any or all of the information contained within this publication. The entire contents are the opinions expressed by the author, which were gathered over years of practical experience and research.

Two final thoughts…first, it is unfortunate but there are people who borrow money, usually via credit cards, with no intention of paying the debt. As a result, many businesses are forced to rely on collection agencies. In fact, the collection business is necessary, for the most part, because of deadbeats who can repay their debts but refuse to do so. Many collection agencies work hard at operating within federal and state laws. They spend a great deal of time and money training their collection agents to follow the FDCPA and various state laws. However, every career field has its bad actors and the collection business is no different. Unfortunately, these bad actors are out there right now breaking the law which is why this book is necessary.

Second, this eGuide is not about getting out of paying valid debts; it's about helping you understand your rights when life's circumstances force you to choose between paying a credit card and survival. It's about providing the information you need to help you deal with debt collectors who cross the line and use illegal and unethical tactics to scare you into paying a debt that is not yours, that you already paid, or that you simply cannot afford to pay right now.

Chapter 1

Introduction

Let me begin by emphasizing two rules…

Rule #1: No matter how far in debt or how broke you are…you still have rights!

Rule #2: Learn to **"Control the Ball"** and, in doing so, you'll reduce your stress and take back control of your life!

<u>Control the Ball</u>

Collectors depend on you not knowing about or understanding your rights. Whenever you are uncertain of your rights…collectors control the ball! Learning about your rights and how to use them, protects you and let's you control the ball.

Unscrupulous collectors use your ignorance against you. They play upon your emotions. They are experts at making you feel helpless and worthless. But, if you know exactly what collectors can and cannot do according to the FDCPA, and other laws, then you'll be in position to fight back when they break the law!

In 1985 I separated from the military and took a job in construction making decent money for the area. I had a home, a car, and several credit cards. I was doing fine until the bottom dropped out of the housing market and construction work dried up. Within weeks I was let go and for a few months lived off my credit cards but they were soon maxed out and, with no job and no way to pay the bills, it didn't take long for the collection calls to start. I was forced out of my home, and after living in my car for awhile, I lost that as well. I was flat broke, had no job, no car, no home, and a ton of bills.

I understand what it means to fall on hard times. I know how it feels when self-esteem drops to an all-time low. We begin thinking terrible things about ourselves. We convince ourselves that we are bad people because we cannot pay our debts. I know what it's like to be so embarrassed about your financial situation, that you'll do anything to hide it from your co-workers, bosses, best friends, neighbors, and even your own family.

Shame and embarrassment are two very powerful emotions that cause us to do just about anything to avoid having our situation exposed. Collectors know this and they are very skilled at tapping into these two emotions. That's why the FDCPA contains specific wording to prohibit collectors from intimidating us using tactics that tap into these emotions.

This guide will help you retain and, if necessary, regain your dignity and self confidence by helping you understand your rights, by giving you the information and tools you need to protect your rights…in short, by showing you how to Control the Ball!

Purpose of this Book

Before we go any further, I want to be clear about the purpose of this book. I wrote it to help people who truly want to pay their debts but, for various reasons, (job loss, divorce, major illness, injury, etc.) are unable to pay them and need help dealing with unethical debt collectors. I did not write this guide to help people get one over on their creditors. Anyone who owes a debt and has the means to pay it should do so.

Before going any further, please take a moment to read the brief overview of the debt and credit protection laws referenced throughout this book. **Click to see Debt and Credit Laws** (pg. 72)

With all the preliminary stuff out of the way, it's time to get down to business. I'll begin by describing the difference between collectors and creditors and then cover legal and illegal tactics. Next, I'll cover valid and invalid debts and discuss how to handle each one. After that, I'll cover how to negotiate settlements, how to properly dispute debts, and what to do when collectors obtain default judgments. Then, I'll talk about wage and bank garnishments and end with a detailed discussion of debt payment plans and how to protect your self when making payment offers.

One thing to keep in mind as you read through this book…the FDCPA makes a clear and legal distinction between debt collectors and creditors collecting a debt.

803(6) Debt Collector

Section 803(6) of the FDCPA defines debt collector as a party "who uses any instrumentality of interstate commerce or the mails in any business, the principal purpose of which is the collection of any debts, or who regularly collects or attempts to collect, directly or indirectly, debts owed or due another."

Notwithstanding the exclusion provided by clause (F) of the last sentence of this paragraph, the term includes any creditor who, in the process of collecting his own debts, uses any name other than his own which would indicate that a third person is collecting or attempting to collect such debts. For the purpose of section 808(6), such term also includes any person who uses any instrumentality of interstate commerce or the mails in any business the principal purpose of which is the enforcement of security interests.

803(6)3 Creditor

Creditors are generally excluded from the definition of "debt collector" to the extent that they collect their own debts in their own name. However, the term specifically applies to "any creditor who, in the process of collecting his own debts, uses any name other than his own which would indicate that a third person is" involved in the collection.

Creditors collecting their own debts are not accountable under the FDCPA; therefore, stop calling or cease and desist letters will not work when trying to stop creditors from harassing you. Some states have debt collection laws very similar to the FDCPA that not only apply to debt collectors; they include creditors collecting debts as well.

Chapter 2

Legal and Illegal Debt Collection Tactics

Collectors use several methods to communicate to you that they are attempting to collect a debt. Some methods are legal while others are not only illegal, they're downright mean. Let's look at the legal methods first:

<u>Legal Notifications</u>

Phone Calls, Letters, Post Cards, Email, and Personal Visits

Section 805(a) of the FDCPA covers collection calls to debtors. Unless you consent or a court order permits, debt collectors may not call:

> At any time or place which is unusual or known to be inconvenient to you. (8 a.m. to 9 p.m. is presumed to be convenient);

> When they know you are represented by an attorney with respect to the debt, unless the attorney fails to respond to their communication in a reasonable time period; and

> At work if they know your employer prohibits such contacts.

Debt collectors may not call at any time, or on any particular day, when they have credible information (from you or elsewhere) that it is inconvenient. If debt collectors do not have such information, a call on Sunday is not per se illegal.

Collection calls are generally restricted to normal business days (Mon – Fri). If this is your normal work schedule, and you inform collectors that calling on Saturday and Sunday is inconvenient, collectors must consider these days as "no call" days. On the other hand, if your normal workdays are Wednesday through Sunday, and collectors know this, then they can reasonably assume calls on Saturday and Sunday are not inconvenient.

First-Time Calls

If a collector's very first call happens to fall on a day that you consider a no-call day, he is not violating the FDCPA because he has not yet been informed of when you consider it inconvenient to call.

However, after being informed, collectors violate the FDCPA if they continue calling on no-call days.

By the way (BTW), telling collectors that every day of the week and/or all times of the day is inconvenient will not work. Although every call from a collector is probably inconvenient, collectors, just like everyone else, has a job to do, so when asked be prepared to provide times and days when you prefer they call.

Calls to Work:

Calls to your work are allowed until you or your employer informs the collector that collection calls are prohibited. Informing collectors of this fact can be verbal or written; either one is enforceable but informing the collector in writing is better. When verbally informing collectors, record the call and be sure to tell the collector you are recording the call. If recording the call is not an option, have someone witness the call and be able to testify that he/she actually heard you say, "My employer prohibits collection calls at work" and he/she actually heard the collector's response .

Calls to Cell Phones

Although the FDCPA prohibits collectors from asking debtors to call long distance or accept collect calls, as of this writing, the Federal Trade Commission (FTC) has not prohibited calls to cell phones. (I personally believe calls to cell phones should be prohibited because many calling plans charge for incoming calls).

However, just because you carry the cell phone with you at all times and in all locations, that does not mean collectors can violate the law… they must still follow the rules concerning inconvenient call days/times and calls to your place of work. It goes for text messaging as well.

Calls to Third Parties

Collectors are allowed to call third parties for the purpose of locating you. However, if the collector already has your location information, then calling third parties under the pretense of locating you violates the FDCPA.

When calling third parties collectors must provide their name, state that they are confirming or correcting location information concerning the consumer (that's you) and, only if expressly requested by the third party, identify their employer. They are not allowed to discuss any additional information, even if asked.

Third parties are friends, neighbors, relatives, parents, children, and employers ...basically anyone other than you and your spouse (I cover the spouse clause later). Collectors are not supposed to discuss your personal information but that is exactly what the bad ones do because they know whoever they speak with will contact you to let you know a collector is looking for you, and they know hearing this from a third party is very embarrassing.

Next time your neighbor (or any third party) says, "I have a message for you from a debt collector," immediately ask, "How do you know it's from a debt collector?" You see, collectors who without being asked, identify themselves as debt collectors, or imply in any way they are debt collectors violate the FDCPA. On the other hand, if your neighbor asked whom the caller worked for, then the collector can legally identify his employer. However, it does bring up the question of a nosey neighbor but that discussion would require another book entirely.

Collectors like to call people (HR department, bosses, coworkers, people from other departments, etc.) at your place of employment until they find someone who is not familiar with the FDCPA or company policy on collection calls. Once they find people willing to talk, collectors ask illegal questions about you and discuss your personal information...also illegal. If this happens, and you become aware of it, you should report the violation to someone in the company who is in a position of authority to take appropriate action to correct the employee who spoke with the collector and to ensure all employees understand and adhere to the FDCPA.

Dunning Letters

This is the official name for collection letters. They usually arrive by mail, but I've received thousands of emails from people who've found dunning notices tacked on doors and gates to their home, their vehicle windshield, their desks at work, and other prominent locations. Some people wrote to tell me the collector hand-delivered the dunning notice and still others had them handed to them by third parties. None of these notification methods are illegal as long as they follow the rules outlined next.

Dunning letters, if not enclosed in an envelope, must not convey its nature to anyone other than the debtor or the debtor's spouse. For instance, tacking a letter on your front door that says "NOTICE TO COLLECT A DEBT" is illegal. Also illegal is sending a letter (or tacking it on your door) that has "debt" or "collector" or any other name that indicates a debt collection business, as the name of the business. The same goes for any envelopes containing dunning letters.

Envelopes must not be transparent or reveal language or symbols indicating a debt collection business. The debt collector's address and business name are permissible as long as they do not contain the words "debt" or "collector" or any other name that indicates a debt collection business.

Post Cards:

Post cards are prohibited by the FDCPA. If you receive a post card, report the violation to your State Attorney General immediately. Also, keep it as evidence in case future legal actions become necessary. In fact, it's a good idea to keep all correspondence from collectors as evidence, including envelopes!

E-mail:

As of this writing I was unable to find any rulings from the Federal Trade Commission (FTC) prohibiting collectors from sending dunning notices by email. So, it is my opinion that this type of notification, if used, must meet the same requirements as dunning letters distributed by regular mail. This is problematic for collectors because all E-mail can be read by people as it works its way through the electronic system.

Although not as effective as calls or letters because you can just delete the message, it does put you on notice that a collector is after you. It also has the added advantage of requesting a read receipt.

This type of notification is dangerous for collectors but advantageous for you because of the paper trail it leaves behind. Some collectors think it's clever to send e-mail with COLLECTION NOTICE or similar text in the subject line or body of the email and courtesy copy the debtor's boss. This is not only a clear violation of the FDCPA, it's just plain stupid. Employers can view employees' E-mail which opens the door for a lawsuit against the collector for violating the FDCPA. So, be sure to save E-mail from collectors.

The FDCPA requires cease and desist demands be put in writing, but it does not specify the letter must be sent via official mail. So, you could reply to a collector's e-mail and state that the collector is to cease and desist contacting you. Just be sure to send the e-mail return read receipt requested and print a copy of the email from your sent box to prove who you sent the letter to and when.

Home/Work Visits:

Although rare, these do occur. When collectors do come to your home or workplace, they cannot violate the FDCPA or any other law. For instance, they are not allowed to show up at your place of employment or in your neighborhood and tell people they are a collector or give any indication they are there to collect a debt.

Although the methods outlined above are all legally acceptable methods for notifying debtors, phone calls are by far the most popular method. In fact, one of the most unsettling moments for many people is getting that very first call from a debt collector.

That First Debt Collection Call – What's legal?

On first contact, collectors are supposed to verify they are speaking to you or your spouse (if married). This is supposed to prevent collectors from discussing your personal information with the housekeeper or any other third party (including your children and parents). By the way…the FDCPA allows collectors to discuss your debt with your spouse even if your spouse is not on the account or even aware of the debt! By spouse I mean legally married…live-in friends do not count!

As of this writing, Colorado, Connecticut, Hawaii, Iowa, Louisiana, Maine, Massachusetts, New York City, Pennsylvania, and South Carolina prohibit collectors from speaking with spouses. To be sure, check with your state attorney general to learn about your state's rules concerning this issue.

As soon as collectors discover they are not speaking with you or your spouse (assuming your state does not prohibit this), they should leave a name and number and request a call back but nothing more. The message should NOT reveal any information, give any indication that the call is from a debt collector or imply any threat. The ONLY exception is when specifically asked; collectors may reveal their employer's name but nothing more!

Once collectors confirm they are speaking with you or your spouse, they should immediately identify their self and explain the reason for the call. If you ask, they must provide the name of the collection company they work for or the creditor they represent (so always ask). But, as you can imagine, most calls don't go like this at all!

Many collectors "Control the Ball" from the start by verifying (but not always) they are speaking with the debtor and then immediately demand full payment of the debt. Even if you ask for their name and the name of their company, many collectors ignore your request and keep pressing for payment. We'll cover how to handle this when we get to illegal tactics.

Note: Collectors often use fake or company-assigned names to protect their privacy. There is nothing illegal about this practice.

Believe it or not, there are quite a few collectors who handle collection calls in a positive, yet forceful and professional manner without becoming abusive or resorting to illegal tactics. Collection calls should really be about two adults working to solve a problem but unfortunately there are collectors who use dirty tricks, abusive language and underhanded tactics…that give all collectors a bad reputation.

I know there are people out there who purposefully run up debt and then skip out on it; collectors call these people deadbeats and rightfully so. But, until collectors establish a debtor as a deadbeat, they should give all debtors the benefit of the doubt, treat them with courtesy, and respect their rights. But, if that were the case, this guide wouldn't be necessary.

Before collectors even pick up the phone, they know most debtors cannot afford to pay the full amount of the debt using just their regular paycheck. Savvy collectors know demanding payments that debtors cannot afford is a waste of time. So, to prevent the conversation from quickly deteriorating into a shouting match, they call armed with plenty of suggestions for coming up with the money.

Collector's weapon of choice is the credit report because it reveals everything they need to know about your financial situation…especially how much credit you have available on your credit cards, home equity line of credit and other loans. Although pulling your credit report and suggesting ways to come up with the money is annoying, it is not illegal. Collectors, who are trying to collect a debt, have a legitimate business purpose for pulling your reports. Here are the most common suggestions collectors make while looking at your credit report:

Use Other Credit Cards: With a credit report in front of them, collectors know the balance and credit limit of every credit card you have;

Take Out a Loan: They especially like suggesting payday loans and title loans but will also suggest refinancing current personal loans and mortgages;

Borrow the Money: They'll insist you borrow from friends, parents, relatives, and so forth;

Cash In or Borrow from Your Life Insurance: Through questions, they'll try to determine the amount of equity in your life insurance policies and then demand you borrow against or use the equity to pay the debt;

Draw from IRA/401K or Other Retirement Fund: Same as above, they try to determine your worth through questions and then demand you withdraw funds to pay the debt.

Make Payments: This is always their last suggestion because taking payments requires time and effort and eats into their profit margin. Collectors are trained to dun for, and accept nothing less than, full payment. Most will refuse to accept anything but one lump-sum payment. If they agree to payments, it's usually two or three payments at most, and they'll insist on payment by automatic withdrawal or postdated checks (more on this under payment plans).

> CAUTION: **The above suggestions are legal…however you are under no legal obligation to agree to any of them!**

But, as you might have guessed, collectors want you to believe, and they are very good at making you believe, that you must do something to come up with the money or else something terrible is going to happen to you! With this in mind and a basic understanding of what collectors can do legally, let's explore what the bad collectors usually do.

Illegal Notifications and Collection Tactics

This section explores illegal and unethical tactics. From this point forward, all information is presented from the point of view that we're dealing with collectors who use illegal tactics to intimidate and scare uninformed debtors into paying.

Calls to Your Home

Calling several times a day even though you've told them over and over you can't pay. If you did agree to a payment plan, they may even call back and tell you their boss refused to accept the plan. This is almost always a lie! (see **good guy – bad guy routine** pg. 43).

Two or more collectors from the same company call (often several times a day) and act as if they are completely unaware of the other collector's call. They'll use some lame excuse, such as the computer doesn't show the other calls, but, rest assured, they know exactly who called and what transpired during that call; they're working you.

They call and leave nasty, threatening messages on your answering machine. Threatening messages are illegal so be sure and keep a copy of the message and report the violation to your state attorney general;

They use abusive and threatening language toward your spouse hoping he or she will convince you to pay up, if for no other reason than to stop the harassment.

They call just before 8 am or just after 9 pm. In blatant cases they'll call around 6:30 – 7:00 am. If you point this out to them, they'll usually claim innocence or claim they're calling from a different time zone or some other weak excuse. Their intent is to catch you at home and to annoy you.

They call and divulge personal information to anyone who answers (children, parents, friends, housekeeper, etc.) and throw in a threat or two for good measure.

Note 1: When collectors have not spoken to the debtor or debtor's spouse, the FDCPA does not prohibit leaving a message on a daily basis that includes a name and number with a request to call back.

Note 2: According to the FTC's published interpretation of the FDCPA, collectors cannot continuously call you. Section 806(5) prohibits contacting the consumer by telephone "repeatedly or continuously with intent to annoy, abuse, or harass any person at the called number." Continuously means making a series of telephone calls, one right after the other. "Repeatedly" means calling with excessive frequency under the circumstances. When collectors have no purposeful reason to call you, but do so, they violate the FDCPA. So, when collectors call and no meaningful conversations occur, it is most definitely harassment! Also, after reaching a payment agreement, calling again before the payment date without any purposeful disclosure of information, is also illegal.

Calls to Your Work

Collectors call several times a day just to interrupt your work and to attract the attention of co-workers and supervisors. Their intent is to embarrass you to the point where you'll pay up just to stop the calls and…perhaps keep your job. This technique is especially effective when you have to be paged or someone has to come find you to take the call.

They threaten to call your boss or the Human Resource department to have you fired or have your wages garnished. Many collectors actually follow through and call and discuss your personal information with these third parties. Whether they threaten to call or actually call does not matter; the threats are illegal and so are the calls to your boss or other third parties. Remember, calling third parties should only occur when the collector is trying to locate you. If collectors already have your work information then they have no legal reason to call any other person at your place of employment.

Calls to Third Parties

The FDCPA allows collectors to contact third parties to obtain location information. However, these calls are only allowed if collectors do not already possess your location and contact information. Collectors may not discuss anything other than location information. ***NO OTHER QUESTIONS ALLOWED!***

However, collectors will call your friends, neighbors, relatives, co-workers, supervisors and just about anyone they can think of to embarrass and intimidate you. Even if they don't discuss your personal information, they know just calling these third parties will cause the third party to contact you. Unethical collectors will reveal enough information so you are embarrassed when the third party does contact you. Again, collectors who call third parties after they already possess your location information violate the FDCPA.

> **NOTE: The definition of third party is anyone other than your spouse.   This includes children, parents, relatives, neighbors, friends, co-workers, subordinates, supervisors, etc.).   The FDCPA does not consider your spouse a third party;   therefore, collectors are free to discuss your debts with your spouse unless your state prohibits it (currently prohibited by Colorado, Connecticut, Hawaii, Iowa, Louisiana, Maine, Massachusetts, New York City, Pennsylvania, and South Carolina)**

Dunning Letters

As stated earlier, dunning letters cannot arrive in transparent envelopes or contain any markings or symbols that indicate the letter (or envelope) is from a debt collector. But, collectors still use some pretty ingenious but illegal methods to intimidate you.

Using letterhead that appears to be from the Internal Revenue Service, other government agencies, attorneys, district courts, and legal or pre-legal departments;

Using words, phrases, terms, and names that imply the letter is from an official government source, an attorney or court or legal department.

Saying or implying legal action is pending when in fact they have not filed any legal paperwork, don't intend to take such action, don't normally take such action, or they are not authorized to take such action. Collectors can only threaten action they have the legal authority to take, and the vast majority of collection agencies have zero legal authority. (For example, stating or implying wage garnishment is illegal since no collector has the authority to take this action. Only judges have this Authority (see note on page 22).

Stating or implying that legal action has already started (when it hasn't) and the only way to stop it is to pay right away.

Making statements such as, "failure to pay this debt will result in your arrest, loss of job, loss of license, garnishment of wages" and so forth.

Note: Most debts are considered a civil matter so the threat of jail is illegal however, in some states failure to pay child support and certain taxes could result in arrest. Check your state laws to be sure.

Threats, Threats and more Threats

Collectors love modern telephone technology because it allows them to hide their identity and to make tracing the call impossible for the average consumer. Technology grants collectors anonymity and so they do and say just about anything to you on the phone because they believe there is nothing you can (or will) do about it. (We'll cover how to deal with this later). Phones allow underhanded collectors to avoid putting things in writing, something they avoid at all costs. You see, with no witnesses; it comes down to your word against their word. Here are some of the most common threats made during collection calls:

Threatening Arrest

Debtor's prison was abolished in the mid-1800s. According to the FDCPA, you cannot be arrested or imprisoned for not paying your debts; therefore, it is flat out illegal to say you will be arrested if you do not pay.

Note 1: I'm not talking about debts incurred as a result of a crime such as tax evasion, credit card fraud, and writing checks with the intent to defraud (see bad checks pg. 70). People who commit these crimes can and

should be arrested and face whatever consequences the courts decide.

Note 2: Many states now have laws that allow the arrest and imprisonment of people who do not pay their child support.

Wage and Bank Account Garnishment

The wage garnishment threat works best on people who are unaware of how the garnishment process works and on people who are afraid to ask for help. All of us would do just about anything to avoid the embarrassment of having the entire human resource department and the people at our local bank see a garnishment order with our name on it.

Although it's true that wages and bank accounts can be garnished, collectors cannot do this on their own! If they are collecting for a creditor, only the creditor can authorize pursuing a court order to garnish wages. If creditors or collectors pursue legal action, you are supposed to be notified, in writing of the date, time, and location of the court hearing.

Note: Federal student loans in default, overdue state and federal taxes and overdue child support being collected by state officials or collectors hired by these officials DO NOT require court orders.

Except for the situations noted above, (student loans, taxes and child support) collectors must first obtain permission from the creditor, or they must own the debt outright, before filing court papers to obtain a judgment. Your wages and bank accounts can only be garnished or seized if your state allows it and only AFTER a court judgment is approved (more on judgments later). Either most states prohibit wage and bank account garnishment outright or they have strict limits on how much can be taken.

Federal law limits wage garnishment to 25 percent of your disposable income except student loans which are limited to 10 percent of your disposable income and child support which can run as high as 60 percent in some states.

Collectors typically purchase debts in huge bundles. These collectors are known as "Junk Debt Buyers" or JDB. These bundled debts come with little or no records, so validating disputed debts can be difficult, if not impossible. Because of this, by just by showing up at a court hearing and disputing the debt, you can usually have the case dismissed, or at least postponed, until the collector properly validates the debt in accordance with the FDCPA.

Also, because of poor record keeping and the age of collection accounts, collectors often find it extremely difficult to validate debts in accordance with the FDCPA. The number one reason for collectors obtaining judgments is debtors who fail to show for court hearings! (See **Default Judgments** pg. 55).

Seizure of Possessions

In many states, personal possessions can be seized; however, collectors must obtain a judgment first and then go through the process of serving all the paperwork necessary to actually take your possessions. They cannot take anything that is collateral for another debt. Most states allow exemptions so certain personal items and property are safe from seizure. Some states even prohibit this entire process.

This can and does happen but not as often as collectors would like you to believe. The time, money, and trouble to actually seize and then sell property make this option prohibitive or at least undesirable for most collectors. Besides, most people who are up to their ears in debt usually don't own anything outright that's worth taking.

You'll be fired

No collector or creditor holds the power to fire you! That decision rests solely with your employer. Ninety-nine percent of the time, employers do not fire people because they receive calls from debt collectors. My goodness, if American employers fired every employee whom they learned was in debt, they'd have to fire most of their workforce!

Some employers, like the military, financial institutions, some government employees, investigators, and so forth have strict rules about financial responsibility. However, even the military must follow certain policies and procedures before discharging (similar to firing) anyone. Protect yourself by knowing your company's policy regarding debt and by letting your supervisor know you are experiencing a problem. You don't have to share everything. But, at least tell your boss enough to gain his or her support just in case a collector does call. In many cases, you'll dispute the debt, so keeping your supervisor informed can diffuse a tense situation and stop the rumor mill.

Finally, don't forget that it's illegal for collectors to discuss your situation with any third party, such as your boss or other employees. When this happens, inform your employer of the FDCPA violation and then report the violation to your State Attorney General.

Embarrassment and Shame

This covers everything from calling third parties to posting your name on a debtor's list. Most people are inherently good and want to do the right thing, but life happens (unemployment, sickness, injury, divorce, and so forth). Because we are inherently good, collectors tap into this part of our emotional nature. First, they try to shame you into paying, and, if that doesn't work, they resort to calling you names, like loser and deadbeat. There is nothing wrong with collectors using our sense of right and wrong to try and get us to pay, but, when it becomes abusive, condescending and degrading, they cross the FDCPA's unfair practices line. By the way, posting names of debtors in ANY public forum violates the FDCPA.

Ruin Your Credit

This is one the most popular threats because we live in a credit-minded society, and any damage to our credit can have devastating results on our ability to purchase things. We work hard to establish our creditworthiness, and the threat of ruining all of our hard work, not to mention our reputation, is enough to scare many into paying. We have laws that help protect our credit. (See **When Collectors Lie to Credit Reporting Agencies** pg. 65).

Using Your Credit Report as Leverage

Just the idea that collectors can pull a credit report rattles most people. But, what is even more surprising is the reason why. Collectors can pull credit reports because according to the Fair Credit Reporting Act (FCRA) they have a "legitimate business purpose," And, if that's not enough, it's highly likely that you agreed to it when you signed the original credit contract.

Credit contracts usually contain a clause with words such as, "You agree that the creditor and any representative or beneficiary can obtain a copy of your credit report should your account become delinquent." Check it out! Go get the credit disclosure statement from any of your creditors (especially from credit card issuers) and read the fine print; I guarantee you'll find the above statement or one very similar.

As soon as collectors start making suggestions such as, "You have credit left on your Visa card..." or "Borrow against your home equity...," you can bet they have a copy of your credit report.

When collectors start making the above suggestions, most people react with disbelief and shock and then become angry and ask, "How did you get my report without my permission?" Collectors love this question because it not only indicates you are unaware of your rights. It also allows them to "Control the Ball."

The typical collector response to the above question is, "I can get information about you any time I want, and there is nothing you can do about it." Because they have your credit report and know all of your personal credit history, this statement deals a powerful psychological blow that collectors count on to keep you off balance.

Credit reports reveal so much information; the balance and credit limits of all our credit cards, mortgages and other loans and which bills are paid or delinquent. When collectors look at our reports, it's like being naked with no way to cover up.

Now that we've looked at the most common threats, let's move on to learning the difference between valid and invalid debts and how to handle each type.

Chapter 3

How to Handle Valid and Invalid Debts

The information in this section assumes that all calls or debt notifications are from debt collectors not creditors. In order to eliminate any confusion, I'll explain the difference between the two and then move on to valid and invalid debts.

Definition of Creditors

Section 803(4) of the FDCPA defines creditor as "any person who offers or extends credit creating a debt or to whom a debt is owed." However, the definition excludes a party who "receives an assignment or transfer of a debt in default solely for the purpose of facilitating collection of such debt for another."

This section of the FDCPA excludes creditors. Thus, creditors collecting their own debts under their own name cannot be sued under the FDCPA. However, creditors lose this protection if, in the process of collecting their own debts, they use any name other than their own, which would indicate that a third person is collecting or attempting to collect such debts.

Just to be clear, creditors who use a different name to collect debts become "Debt Collectors" and thus must adhere to the FDCPA. They can be sued for violating it.

Nowadays creditors often circumvent the FDCPA by establishing their own in-house collections department. Employees working in internal collection departments are collecting on behalf of the creditor and are therefore exempt from the FDCPA. Some creditors use this loophole to allow (even encourage) employees to use collection tactics that are otherwise prohibited by the FDCPA. However, creditors cannot just do whatever they want. They can be held accountable under other federal and state creditor and/or collection and banking laws. Many states have enacted their own version of the Fair Debt Collection Act.

Definition of Debt Collectors

Debt Collectors fall into two categories:

They ***DO NOT*** own the debt! So, they collect on behalf of (working for) the original creditor; or

They own the debt and are collecting for themselves or the collection agency for which they work.

Section 803(6) of the FDCPA defines debt collector as "a party who uses any instrumentality of interstate commerce or the mails in any business, the principal purpose of which is the collection of any debts, or who regularly collects or attempts to collect, directly or indirectly, debts owed or due another."

For the purpose of section 803(6), this term also includes any person who uses any instrumentality of interstate commerce or the mails in any business the principal purpose of which is the enforcement of security interests.

The term includes:

Employees of a debt collection business, including a corporation, partnership, or other entity whose business is the collection of debts owed another.

A firm that regularly collects overdue rent on behalf of real estate owners, or periodic assessments on behalf of condominium associations, because it "regularly collects . . . debts owed or due another."

A party based in the United States who collects debts owed by consumers residing outside the United States because he "uses . . . the mails" in the collection business. The residence of the debtor is irrelevant.

A firm that collects debts in its own name for a creditor, solely by mechanical techniques, such as placing phone calls with prerecorded messages and recording consumer responses, or making computer-generated mailings.

An attorney or law firm whose efforts to collect consumer debts on behalf of its clients regularly include activities traditionally associated with debt collection, such as sending demand letters (dunning notices) or making collection telephone calls to the consumer. However, an attorney is not considered to be a debt collector simply because he responds to an inquiry from the consumer following the filing of a lawsuit.

See this page for in-depth information on creditor and collector exemptions:
http://www.fair-debt-collection.com/rules/fair-debt-collection-act.html

Now that we have a working definition of creditor and collector, let's move on to defining valid and invalid debts and learning how to handle each type.

Handling Valid and Invalid Debts

Valid Debts

Debts are either valid or invalid; there is no "gray" area. Let me say that again; debts can only be valid or invalid! Valid debts are debts that:

You are absolutely certain you owe; and

The amount demanded is correct!

Note: The FDCPA does not require a reason to dispute a debt; however, you should always act in good faith.

Do not misunderstand what I am saying here! I am not advocating disputing debts in order to get out of paying them. On the contrary, if you owe the debt and the amount stated, and you can afford to pay the debt, then you're duty bound to pay it.

But, when it comes to identification and record keeping there are just too many mistakes made by creditors and collectors therefore, if you have any doubt about the validity of a debt, dispute it!

Besides identification and record-keeping mistakes, collectors often add illegal fees and interest to debts. Because of this fact alone, always dispute debts that you believe to be invalid. Doing so protects your rights under the FDCPA and…in cases where collectors do validate a debt, you will know the debt is valid and, should you decide to pay, you will not have to pay one penny more than necessary to clear the debt.

Let me clarify my statement, "*should you decide to pay*." I've seen people who have had a run of bad luck and living on just a few hundred dollars a month try to pay all debts rather than feed and shelter their family. The truth is personal financial situations, such as layoffs, divorces; injuries, medical emergencies, and so forth force us to choose between feeding our family and paying our debts. When it comes down to feeding your children or paying a credit card debt, the choice is clear; feed your children. Creditors, who offer credit cards, know this is the choice you'll make and it's the risk they take…that's why they're called "Unsecured Debts."

Invalid Debts

There are many reasons for debts to be considered invalid. The most common are:

Wrong Person, Wrong Amount, Wrong Account, or Previously Paid or Settled:

This happens more often than people realize. Given the population of this country and the millions of credit (and debt) accounts, it's easy to see why collectors end up with information that is sketchy at best. Records are always being lost, misplaced, deleted or destroyed and debts are constantly being assigned to the wrong account because of similar names or other data entry errors.

Collectors often take a "shot in the dark" when they call or send dunning notices. They may or may not know if you are the right person, but in order to control the ball, they operate from the position that you are the right person and leave it up to you to prove otherwise.

A typical tactic is to call and demand you tell them your social security number (SSAN) to verify your identity. NEVER provide this information to strangers. Instead, have the caller tell you the number they have, and then you can confirm it's your number, or, if it's not your SSAN, tell them they have the wrong person. Understand that I'm not advocating lying. If they provide the right social security number or other personal information, you should answer truthfully.

Creditor Dispute

It's not uncommon for creditors to send (or sell) accounts to third-party collectors even though you dispute the debt. Some companies are so big and/or unorganized that one area does not talk to the other and mistakes happen and most of these mistakes can be traced to miscommunication or a lack of communication. All creditors have internal policies for handling debts…some keep trying to collect a debt for months while others will attempt once or twice and then turn the account over to collections.

When disputing a debt with a creditor or collector, always protect yourself by disputing the debt in writing and by keeping copies of your efforts. To place an account in dispute, use this **sample initial dispute letter** (pg. 90). Send the letter to whoever is trying to collect the debt; just be sure to change the text of the letter to reflect your information and, if applicable, the dates of other disputes on the same account.

Already Paid the Debt

Believe it or not this happens all the time. You paid a debt (or settled it) with the creditor or another collector, and then, months or even years later, collectors contact you claiming you still owe all or some of the original debt. Use this sample **Previously Paid Debt Letter** (pg. 86) or this sample **Previously Settled Letter** (pg. 87) to send to whoever is trying to collect a debt.

Debt was discharged in Bankruptcy

Debts discharged in bankruptcy are no longer collectable from the person granted the discharge. Attempts to collect discharged debts violate the FDCPA and bankruptcy laws. However, if someone else was responsible for the debt as well (usually a spouse, ex-spouse or parent) and he or she was not included in the bankruptcy, then he or she may be held accountable for the debt. There are many state-specific rules about collecting debts from alternate account holders and spouses…always verify state rules through your State Attorney General.

Now that we've covered valid and invalid debts, let's look at valid debts and your options. Remember, these options assume you are absolutely certain the debt is valid.

Valid Debts—Options and Choices:

You know my opinion, if the debt is valid and you can pay it, you should do so. Whether or not you pay a valid debt is a personal decision that only you can make. Therefore, the following information is intended to help you make an informed decision.

The Statute of Limitations (SoL)

All states have SoL laws that define when a debt expires. When the SoL expires, it means the time limit for collectors and creditors to obtain court judgments or garnishments has expired. In other words, courts (if informed by you of the expired SoL) cannot be used to enforce the collection of the expired debt.

> **WARNING! Collectors can (and will) still try to collect valid debts using other legal means, such as phone calls and dunning letters…they do this all the time! Although they can attempt to collect expired debts for as long as they want, without the power of a court ordered judgment, collectors have very little hope of collecting expired debts because they have no legal method of forcing you to pay.**

As I stated earlier, all states have their own Statute of Limitations for various types of debts. For instance, most credit card debt expires after 4-6 years, bounced checks typically expire after 2-3 years, contracts typically run from 5-10 years and judgments can last up to 21 years (but in most states the judgment must be renewed at the 6-10 year point).

The Statutes of Limitations exist for a very good reason; at some point in time, people must be able to get on with their lives. Once a debt expires it becomes a personal choice whether to pay it or not. If you choose to pay, see the section on debt payments and negotiations. If you choose not to pay, use this sample **Expired Statute of Limitations Letter** (pg. 88) to let collectors know that you are aware of the SoL and will use it as your defense should they decide to pursue legal action. (See **Statutes of Limitations** (pg. 100) for more information.

> **WARNING! In many states making a payment or making a promise to pay in writing resets the SoL. Collectors (at least the well trained ones) know this, so**

they work very hard at getting you to make a payment because even a small token payment can reset the SoL. Then, with proof of your payment or your promise to pay in hand, collectors can take the case to court and win a judgment against you. (See Statutes of Limitations **(pg. 100) for more information.**

Just to be clear…collectors can still try and collect valid debts that have expired; they just can't use the courts (if you inform the court) to enforce their collection efforts. Sending the expired SoL letter makes collectors aware that you know your rights and will use them to defend yourself.

Making Periodic Payments

For most of us, making periodic payments is about the only way we can pay off a debt. Whenever possible, payments should be to the original creditor, rather than to a collector hired by the creditor. However, some creditors refuse to work with debtors once the account is sent to collections, so in these cases, if you wish to pay the debt, you'll have to work with and make payments through the collector.

> IMPORTANT: **The FDCPA requires collectors to credit your payments to the account or accounts that you designate. If you owe several debts, always designate in writing which account, or accounts, the payment is for and the amount to be applied toward each account. Be very specific when designating accounts and amounts!**

Periodic payments are whatever timeframe you and the collector (or creditor) agrees to such as weekly, every other week, monthly or some other designated period of time. Only offer to pay what you can truly afford and ALWAYS get the payment agreement in writing BEFORE paying anything!

NEVER use verbal agreements as proof that your payment offer has been accepted. Even if you've already made one or more payments before reading this guide, put the payment agreement in writing and send the letter return receipt requested.

You may be tempted to include the first payment as a show of "good faith" but weigh this decision carefully. If you're sending a payment agreement to the creditor, then including a payment is probably a good idea. Sending money to collectors without a written and accepted payment agreement is foolish.

If the collector is working for the creditor, verify with the creditor exactly what the collector is authorized to do and what terms the creditor will accept. Again, never agree to any terms that you cannot afford. See the section on **Payment Offers** (Pg. 30) and then use this sample **Payment Offer/Agreement Letter** (Pg. 75)

Finally, watch out for fraud! There have been many cases of so-called collectors accepting payments and never applying the money toward the balance. Record keeping is extremely important so ALWAYS PUT THINGS IN WRITING AND KEEP ACCURATE RECORDS!

I cannot afford to pay anything

Whether the situation is temporary or permanent, IF the debt is valid, send the creditor a letter outlining your situation. If the situation is temporary, offer to contact the creditor as soon as your financial situation improves. Providing a future timeframe for payments demonstrates "good faith" on your part. Even if you have to guess at when you'll be able to start paying, it's a good idea to include a future date.

On the other hand, if your situation is permanent such as permanent disability, then you must be crystal clear about this in your letter. This lets creditors (and collectors) know the account is not worth pursuing. Although the more aggressive collectors may still pursue it, if you've been honest, they'll soon discover they are wasting their time and move on to greener pastures. (Use this sample **Judgment Proof Letter** pg. 83).

I want to settle

In this paragraph, settling a debt means paying less than the amount owed. There are only two payment methods to settle debts: lump-sum payment and periodic payments. Obviously creditors, and especially collectors, prefer one large payment, but, depending on the amount of the settlement, they will generally accept more than one payment. On small debts expect to make one payment, maybe two at the most. On larger debts, payments can last several months. See the section on **Settlements and How to Negotiate Them (Pg. 41)**

I refuse to pay:

First, in my opinion there is only one true reason for refusing to pay a valid debt; your current financial situation won't allow it! However, if you just flat out refuse to pay a valid debt, then I do not recommend sending letters that indicate this or discussing the issue with anyone, especially collectors. Making this choice may come back to haunt you, so consider this decision carefully.

Note: Two of the previous options are vital and deserve in-depth explanations. We'll cover payment offers first and then go over settlements in detail.

How to Make Payment Offers

First and foremost ALWAYS put your offer in writing! Just as important, NEVER promise to pay more than you can truly afford. Breaking either rule is a recipe for disaster.

I don't recommend making payment offers or agreements over the phone for three reasons:

First, chances are pretty high that you're being pressured to pay, and, under the emotional strain, you'll more than likely agree to pay more than you can afford.

Second, although verbal agreements are legal and binding in some states, you do not have the time, emotional energy or money to fight over what was agreed upon so why put yourself through all that.

Third, I've seen it happen time and time again; you send several payments, and, just when you think the debt is paid off, the collector calls and says you still owe more! Without a written agreement outlining the debt and amount owed…you have a fight on your hands.

If you feel comfortable with your negotiating skills and decide to make a verbal agreement over the phone, please protect yourself, immediately put the agreement in writing and send it to the creditor or collector it to the creditor or collector, return receipt requested.

If you're not comfortable negotiating this kind of issue (and most of us are not), then refuse to agree to anything. Tell them you need to look at your budget before committing to anything. This should be a true statement, so say it with conviction! Never agree to pay anything until after you've looked at your financial situation in a calm and rational manner. Only then will you be able to make a "Good Faith" payment offer that you can live with and that will stand up in court. Consider the following points _BEFORE_ making payment offers:

Has the Statute of Limitations expired? If so, you can choose to not pay the debt.

How much can you afford this month, next month and every month until the debt is paid?

What time of the year is it? Are taxes coming due, any special occasions coming up? Consider and plan for bills that come due only a couple times a year. What about heating or cooling bills and other utilities; do they fluctuate up and down? If you have school-age children, and school is about to start, consider school supplies, clothing and so forth.

Are you putting anything into savings for emergencies? If not, start today. Always put something away even if it's just a few dollars. Everyone needs an emergency fund for unexpected expenses.

How much can you truly offer (or should pay)?

It's usually counterproductive to offer an extremely small amount on debts that can legally accumulate interest because the payment usually covers only the interest thus you never make any headway in paying down the debt.

Also, if you're operating on an extremely tight budget and you agree to pay a few dollars a month, you've committed to months of struggling to make each payment. Given your tight budget, if your offer is accepted (that's a big if), your chances of missing a payment is high. Missing a payment opens the door for collectors to seek a judgment because you've broken two promises; the original contract with the creditor and now your own written promissory note.

Collectors seldom accept small payments because it eats into their profit margin. Although collectors threaten court action if your payment is too small, they seldom follow through (making the threat illegal) because they know the chances of actually collecting anything are pretty slim.

How much is 25 percent of your disposable income? If creditors (and collectors who own the debt) win a court judgment, they can request wage garnishment (if your state allows such action). Under federal and most state law, garnishment can take up to 25 percent of your disposable income. Payment offers that are way below this amount might cause some creditors and collectors to try for a judgment and then garnish your wages. After all, if 25 percent is more than what you're offering to pay, collectors may pursue court action if you make enough money to make it worth their time and effort to go to court.

IMPORTANT NOTE: Not all states allow wage garnishment. Disposable income is after-tax income that is officially calculated as the difference between personal income and personal tax and non-tax payments (whatever money you have left after paying all required taxes and national insurances). Personal tax and non-tax payments are about 15 percent of personal income, which makes disposable personal income about 85 percent of personal income.

Put another way, disposable income is that portion of an individual's income (wages and salaries, interest and dividend payments from financial assets, and rents and net profits from businesses as well as capital gains on real or financial assets) over which the recipient has complete discretion.

Finally, the 25 percent is the combined total of one or more garnishments. For instance, if a student loan is already garnishing 10 percent (10% is the federal limit) of your disposable income then a collector could only get 15 percent of the rest of your disposable income. In this case, offering payments equal to 15 percent of your disposable income is a legitimate offer.

Are you judgment-proof?

Judgment-proof is the commonly used term but a more accurate term is "execution-proof"! Even after creditors and debt collectors win lawsuits, they still have to collect the debt (courts do not collect debts). So, if you're penniless, on disability or social security and have no income (other than income that is exempt from garnishment) then you're insulated not from judgment but from execution of the judgment (the actual collection of the debt). Depending on the nature of your situation, you may be temporarily or permanently judgment-proof. Use this sample **Judgment Proof Letter** (Pg. 83) to let collectors know about your situation.

You may be judgment-proof during periods of unemployment or while drawing disability pay or disability retired pay. You are also judgment-proof if you have no assets such as home, car, land, and other big-ticket items. In other words, you have no money and can prove it!

Generally, Social Security benefits are exempt from execution, levy, attachment, garnishment, or other legal process, or from the operation of any bankruptcy or insolvency law. The exceptions are for current and back child support payments, overdue taxes and other monies owed to the state or federal government.

Most state-paid and private disability insurance payments are exempt from garnishment. The exceptions are for current and back child support payments and overdue taxes. Also, most retired disability pay is exempt, but it's best to call your State Attorney General's consumer protection division and ask about your particular situation.

If you become employed again or gain some other form of income and the new income pays enough to make payments, you can lose your "judgment proof" status. If that happens and you decide to pay the debt, be proactive and negotiate a reduced payoff rather than risk a court-ordered judgment.

If you cannot offer a reasonable amount, it's best to tell creditors up front and offer to contact them when/if your financial situation improves.

So what constitutes a reasonable payment amount? It depends on the amount of the debt. Offering to pay $10 a month on a $100 debt is reasonable. Offering the same amount on a $10,000 debt is not.

Use the 25 percent garnishment rule and your best judgment to come up with a payment amount. The higher the debt, the higher the payment offer should be. However, regardless of the amount of debt, payment offers should be enough to cover interest (if interest is allowed to be added to the debt) and some of the principle balance. There is no point in throwing your money away on an account that accrues more interest than your payment covers. Consider putting the money in savings and when you have enough, use it to make a settlement offer.

> **Important Note: When offering payments to collectors and creditors, always negotiate the elimination of interest accruing.**

On especially tight budgets, show your "Good Faith" effort to resolve the issue by offering an amount you can afford and can prove that is all you can afford. BTW, offering small monthly payments when you can clearly afford more is not acting in "Good Faith" and may hurt your case if you were to end up in court.

If creditors and collectors get the feeling (or can see from your credit reports) that you can clearly afford more, it's a good bet they'll try for a judgment and then garnish your wages and/or seize your assets. Of course only you know where your money goes and not everything we spend our money on shows up in our credit reports so just because they have your report, don't let that influence your decision…decide based on what you can actually afford.

Some final thoughts on payment agreements:

ALWAYS put payment agreements in writing and send them return receipt requested. Use this sample **Debt Payment Offer/Agreement Letter** (Pg. 75)

Keep accurate records! This means keeping copies of all payment instruments and mail receipts. It also means keeping all correspondence from creditors and collectors including envelopes (contains postmark) and copies of all letters you send. Finally, record all phone conversations either using a recording device or by writing down the times and dates of calls and the gist of the conversation. Although over 40 states allow recording calls without telling the caller you are doing so…always inform the caller at the beginning of the call that you are recording the call. This protects you and helps you Control the Ball!

Never use personal checks to pay collectors! Sending personal checks to collectors gives them all the information they need to seize the funds in your bank account (the name of your banking institution, routing numbers, and, of course, your account number (although they can only do this after obtaining a judgment, you've made their job much easier).

> **Special Note: If you insist on using personal checks, open an account in a different bank (not a branch of your primary bank) and deposit just enough funds to cover your payment each month. This keeps your primary bank information safe and prevents collectors from taking more than the agreed-upon payment (yes collectors have been known to get away with running checks through twice). Also, only put your first name, last name, and post office box number on the checks.**

Security Tip: DO NOT print your middle name (if you have one) on your checks. Sign the bank's signature card and your checks using your middle initial. Because thieves do not know your middle initial, they can only sign checks using your first and last name. However, your bank knows that you sign using your middle initial thus giving some protection against fraud.

Never agree to postdated checks! It's true the FDCPA allows collectors to request postdated checks, but notice I said "request, not require!" Also, just because the FDCPA allows collectors to ask, you are not obligated to pay by post-dated checks! In order to get some payment on the debt, collectors will often agree verbally to your payment plan if you pay by postdated checks--DON'T DO IT!

Section 808(4) prohibits depositing a postdated check prior to its date, and section 808(2) prohibits (banks) from accepting a check postdated by more than five days, unless timely written notice is given to the consumer prior to deposit. This means banks are not supposed to accept checks prior to their date unless the collector has notified you that he intends to deposit (or cash) the check early.

It's nice that the FDCPA contains such a rule, but it still does not prevent collectors from depositing postdated checks early or banks from accepting them; this goes on every day! Once this happens, the consequences can be devastating because your other outstanding checks start bouncing all over the place. Although there are procedures for recovering your money and eliminating the non-sufficient fund (NSF) charges, enforcing the procedures takes time, energy, and money. Why put yourself through all that…just don't use post-dated checks!

Never agree to automatic bank account withdrawals. This is worse than postdated checks!! Not only have you given collectors your personal bank account information, you've given them permission to take money out of your account!

I've lost count of the number of times people have told me their collector withdrew the amount early, withdrew more than the agreed-upon amount, or withdrew the same amount a week or two later on a monthly payment agreement. Yes! There are procedures for recovering your money, but while you're working through the mounds of paperwork, the collector still has your money!

Collectors may negotiate with you, and even accept settlement offers, but only if they can get the amount they desire all at once or in just a payment or two. Put all settlements in writing, and get the collector's signed acceptance BEFORE paying anything.

Collectors seldom agree to payment agreements over the phone because they are trained not to accept anything less than the full amount. If they do accept your offer, get it in writing BEFORE paying. Otherwise, they may accept your payments for a while but then demand more money, and, without a payment agreement, you are on very shaky ground and the collector knows it.

So, again, put your offer in writing and send it to collectors via return receipt requested. Although they may still refuse your offer, you've made a "good faith effort" and have official proof of your efforts. This can go a long way toward swaying the judge in your favor, should you get hauled into court.

IMPORTANT: Contrary to popular belief, there is no law that says, "When collectors refuse your offer, the debt is wiped out." There is a rule under the Uniformed Commercial Code that allows this in relation to tendered payments (checks, bank drafts and so forth), but the rule does NOT apply to debts covered under the FDCPA.

Finally, after paying off the debt, KEEP ALL records for a minimum of 15 years! Yes! I said 15 years! Creditors and collectors seldom keep accurate records, so old debts have a way of resurfacing time and again, even years later. When that happens, your best defense will be accurate records.

With tips and techniques for payment offers and record keeping covered; let's look at settlements and how to negotiate them and what to do once you've reached an agreement.

Settlements and How to Negotiate Them

The only rule when it comes to settling old debts is there is no rule! It's all about negotiating!

You may be wondering, "Rather than settle, is it better to pay a debt in full?" This next section explores several issues to consider before settling and some negotiating principles.

Should I Settle?

First consideration: "How old is the debt?" Wanting to pay the debt in full is admirable, but this option should only be a considered when paying the original creditor. Otherwise you're just lining the pockets of whichever collector got lucky enough to buy the debt just when you're financially able (and willing) to pay the entire thing off.

Debts are bought and sold every day, and each time your debt is sold, the price paid for it declines significantly. If you pay off a $10,000 debt to the fifth Junk Debt Buyer who buys your debt, you are probably paying $9,900 too much!

Second consideration; "Would paying this off improve my credit rating?" If the debt is old and/or being collected by a debt collector, then chances are extremely high that your credit has already sustained damage. Once the damage is done, paying the debt in full will not significantly improve your credit score. Besides, paying debts in full can take months, even years, so, in spite of your efforts, until the debt is paid in full, your credit reports will still report the debts as delinquent. And don't forget, some debts can be reported for up to seven years after they're paid or settled.

Third consideration: This also involves your "Credit Rating!" Regardless of how bad your credit is, the words "debt settled" are always better than the more negative "judgment"! At some point you'll want to rebuild your credit and settling shows you took action to resolve the issue while judgment indicates court action. With that said, consider this issue carefully! (*See fourth consideration*)

Fourth Consideration: If you are trying to get a mortgage or refinance your current home, then you may have no choice but to pay off an old debt. Mortgage lenders often insist on you paying off delinquent debts (especially judgments) listed on your credit reports before authorizing mortgages or refinance loans. Keep in mind that judgments can be negotiated; even new ones! So, if you plan to pay off a judgment in order to obtain a mortgage or similar credit, just know that you don't always have to pay the full amount of the judgment to clear it as long as the person who owns the judgment is willing to accept a lesser amount AND report the debt as paid.

If, after considering the above points, you decide settling is the right way to go, then the next logical questions are, "How much should I settle for and what goes on or comes off my credit report?"

How much should I settle for is not an easy question to answer because there are so many variables. However, knowing and considering the following information can help you arrive at a ballpark figure.

Who owns the debt?

If the original creditor still owns the debt, then the collector may or may not be authorized to accept a settlement. ALWAYS ask this question! But, even if they are authorized to accept settlements, collectors often demand full payment without mentioning settling is an option. Settlement is always a possibility on delinquent debts!

> **Special Note: Collectors violate Section 807 (10.3) of the FDCPA when they tell you the creditor will only accept full payment when they know otherwise. Contact the creditor and ask what they will accept for a payment plan and be sure to tell them the collector they hired is misrepresenting them and violating the FDCPA. Remember, the FDCPA gives you the right to NOT deal with collectors but in order to do so, you must follow the FDCPA rules to protect this right!**

If the debt is old, you can bet the creditor sold it to a collector who paid much less than the balance due. If the collector owns the debt, then the original creditor is out of the picture (except for validating the debt when requested), so paying it now will only make the collector richer while doing little or nothing for your credit.

Assuming the creditor still owns the debt, and assuming the Statute of Limitations (SoL) has not expired or you still want to pay the debt even if it has expired, then a good rule of thumb is the "older a debt the lower the settlement". For more information on the SoL (See the **Statute of Limitations** pg. 100).

On really old debts it's highly likely you're dealing with collectors who own the rights to collect the debt but are several times removed from the original creditor. Chances are the collector paid pennies on the dollar for your debt. Imagine purchasing a $1,000 debt for just 10 bucks and then getting someone to pay you the full $1,000 plus collection fees. That's quite a return for a $10 investment and the reason why Junk Debt Buying is a billion-dollar business!

One Payment vs. Several Payments

If you can make one lump-sum payment, then you have an excellent chance of negotiating a very low settlement. Even making two or three payments gives you a chance of negotiating a decent settlement. As a general rule, "more payments equal higher settlements."

Even if you have to make several payments, all is not lost! Having to make several payments may erode some of your negotiating power, but it does not eliminate it. Just remember creditors and collectors are happy to get something even if it's less than half of what you owe. Something is better than nothing is, so make an offer and see what happens. Put your offer in writing!

What about my Credit Report

Now is the time to negotiate what will be reported or, if already reported, removed or changed in your credit reports. You hold all the cards (cash) at this point, so negotiate to have all negative information related to the debt in question removed from your credit reports. Remember, get this in writing.

The above information should help you decide what to offer. Remember the older the debt, the lower the offer. A good starting place for negotiating a settlement is no more than 10 cents on the dollar. If you're comfortable negotiating over the phone, go ahead and make the offer but remember to get the final agreement in writing BEFORE paying anything. Use this sample **Settlement Offer Letter** (Pg. 84). Even if you're not comfortable negotiating over the phone, you can still use the letter; just modify the wording to fit your offer.

Negotiating a Settlement You Can Live With

First, recognize that you are negotiating from a position of power! Unless you pay, collectors get nothing, so use your position power to negotiate your best deal.

A good place to start is at the bottom! As I stated before, the older the debt, the less you should offer. So offer a ridiculously low amount and see what happens. Whether their reaction is laughter or anger, remain calm and wait (or ask) for a counter offer.

Of course there is always the possibility they'll accept your first offer. If they do, you're golden; just get the offer in writing BEFORE paying anything. Collectors know before calling you that their chances of collecting a lump sum payment is pretty slim, so when you offer it, some will jump at the chance because anything is better than nothing is. But I cannot emphasize this enough…DO NOT pay anything until you have it in writing. Collectors have been known to easily agree to your low offer, take your payment and then come after you for the rest…prevent this and protect yourself by putting the agreement in writing!

Second, NEVER accept their first offer. Experts estimate that as much as 75 percent of our communication comes from our nonverbal body language: gestures, tone of voice, and rate of speech, eye contact and so forth. Anyone can tell, just by looking at people when they speak, if they are being sincere. On the phone, collectors cannot see us, so they must rely on the tone of our voice, and how quickly (or slowly) we talk.

Collectors, at least the really good ones, become very good at listening for verbal clues. They use these clues to judge your mood and attitude and whether or not you're scared or intimidated. So, watch what you say and how you say it. Don't give them reason to believe they are in control. Remember, "Control the Ball."

When they make their first counter offer, remain calm! They may say they have a copy of your credit report and know you can afford it but don't flinch and definitely DON'T agree or disagree with their statement. Remember, only you know where your money goes so don't reveal this information! Instead, say you have copies of your reports too (if you don't have one less than six months old, get one now) and you are disputing your reports because they are inaccurate. Don't elaborate on what's accurate, even if asked!

Third, use their first offer as a starting point to counteroffer. Even if the offer is well below what you are prepared to pay, never say yes because the opening offer is what collectors are hoping to get; it is NOT their bottom line!

Let me explain…Let's say a collector claims you owe the creditor $1,000 but right away offers to settle for $600 if you pay today. You might be thinking, "Wow, I just saved $400!" However, you should be thinking, "I wonder how much more I can save, and why did he just give up $400 so quickly?" The answer is the amount of profit the collector is willing to accept. Remember, collectors buy old debts for pennies on the dollar so, do you really want to pay a collector $600 for a debt he bought for only $50?

Fourth, never give up more than your bottom line. Before you start negotiating, decide on your bottom line, the absolute maximum dollar figure you can afford and that you're willing to pay. Never go over this figure no matter how much pressure you feel.

Try to get collectors to make the first offer. Say something like, "I might be willing to settle if the price is right. What do you think would be fair?" Getting them to offer first tells you how much negotiating range you have to work with. If, after stating the above, collectors don't make an offer, be straightforward and ask them for one. Just asking this question throws inexperienced (and some experienced) collectors off balance because they're just not used to dealing with people who know how to control the ball or who are actually willing to pay.

Don't expect collectors to "throw the ball back"! Instead, expect them to hold the ball and say, "You're in no position to negotiate. Either pay up or face legal action!" The part about the legal action may or may not be true, and it may even be an illegal threat; however, the "being in no position" part is completely false.

They'd like you to believe you have no power, but you actually control all the power because you are the one who decides to pay and how much. You even have the FDCPA on your side! When collectors decide not to cooperate, you have the right to terminate the relationship, and there is nothing they can do about it. Don't let the "You're not in a position to negotiate!" rattle you. By the way, there is nothing in the FDCPA compelling you to cooperate with collectors!

Ignore the, "You're in no position to negotiate" comment and calmly state, "Actually, I am in a position to negotiate because unless we come to an agreement you won't get paid!" Then ask if they want to negotiate or not. If collectors refuse to work with you, end the conversation; it's their loss not yours – never forget that!

Making and receiving the first offer is just the beginning, so do not give up too much too quickly. Everything you say (it's all about verbal communication) is a signal, a verbal clue that helps or hinders a collector's ability to read you and control the ball. Be sure to send the right signals: confidence, persistence, and sincerity. Smile while on the phone; it really does comes through as confidence, and it drives collectors batty.

Let's say that before beginning negotiations on a $1,000 debt you decide $400 is the most you're willing to pay, but $300 would be even better. You offer to pay $100 and the collector counters with $700.

Make your next offer $180 (original $100 plus $80). No matter what the collector offers, make your subsequent offers progressively smaller; ($180 + $60 = $240), ($240 + $40 = $280), and so forth. Using progressively smaller amounts signals to the collector that you are reaching your bottom line. In our example, the final offer would be $300 ($100 + $80 + $60 + $40 + $20)—$100 less than you were willing to pay and right where you hoped to be.

Fifth, before agreeing to an offer, always ask, "What can you do for me?" Let's say you've reached an agreement to pay $300 and the collector says, "I can only accept this offer if you pay by close of business today." You must reply, "If I do that for you, what can you do for me?"

The collector might say, "I won't sue you!" or say "Nothing!" Ignore the behavior and ask again, "Let's not throw away a good deal, I'm willing to pay today, why aren't you willing to do something for me"? On the other hand, the collector might say, "I'll knock another $25 off the deal." You'll never know unless you ask, so ALWAYS ASK! Remember; get this in writing before paying!

Call their bluff on the "Good Guy / Bad Guy" routine.

If you're reading this guide, you've probably already experienced the collector's good guy / bad guy routine. It goes something like this:

A collector calls and claims he wants to work with you. After several minutes of pleasant conversation, he is not even close to a resolution, so he ends the call. A short while later a different collector, from the same company, calls and acts as though he is the first guy's boss (but is more than likely a co-worker).

This guy is mean and nasty! During the conversation you try to explain (several times) that you just don't have the money, but there is just no reasoning with him. He just keeps demanding immediate payment and calling you despicable names, some of which you've never heard before. After insisting that you cannot meet his demands, he ends the call with a threat to call your boss in the morning to have your wages garnished or have you fired (which are lies and illegal threats).

A couple of hours go by giving you plenty of time to talk yourself into being really scared, and suddenly the first collector calls again. He says, "I'm sorry about my boss calling you. I can usually control him, but this time he blew up when he realized you were refusing to cooperate (even though you weren't). I think he's really going to call your boss, but if we can work something out right now, I'm sure I can convince him not to make that call."

Don't fall for it! You were cooperating; they just weren't listening. Recognize what's happening and call him on it. Say, "You don't really think I'm going to fall for that old good guy/bad guy routine do you?" Expect him to deny it, but you can also expect no more calls from his so-called boss. Remember, you do not have to work with him; if he wants to get paid he has to work with you.

You can even use your own good guy/bad guy routine, and you don't even need a real bad guy. You can make one up by saying, "I'd like to consider your offer, but I just can't spend a dime without checking with my spouse (or someone else) first." Build this bad guy up to be the equivalent of their mean and nasty collector bad guy.

Remember, when it comes to settling old debts, the only rule is there is no rule. It's all about negotiating! Just remember to always **GET THE SETTLEMENT IN WRITING** before sending any money and keep copies of everything.

So far we've talked about valid and invalid debts, negotiating settlements and payment plans. Now it's time to take a closer look at the steps for disputing invalid debts.

Chapter 4

Disputing Invalid Debts

Knowledge is power! Collectors hate running up against informed debtors because they can't use the "fear of the unknown," to intimidate them. People who know their FDCPA rights have more power than they realize. I receive letters all the time from people describing their feeling of power (and freedom from worry) after finally standing up to collectors who try to bully them with illegal tactics.

It's often simple things, like knowing what collectors are required to do during their initial contact, what they can and cannot do to you from a legal standpoint, and what recourse you have if they do violate the law. Being able to tell collectors they are violating the law is a vital part of controlling the ball, just as knowing how to properly dispute debts is central to protecting your rights.

Handling That First Collection Call

Above all, remain calm so you can respond appropriately, regardless of how the collector behaves. Believe it or not, collection calls for newbie collection agents can be quite stressful and emotional. So, in order to "control the ball" they use collection scripts.

This helps new collectors stay focused on the task of getting you to pay up. Although seasoned (experienced) collectors don't necessarily rely on a script, they still follow the same basic formula as the beginner. Take a look at this typical **Debt Collection Script** (pg. 76) and then return here to continue learning how to handle that first call.

Welcome back! Now that you know about collection scripts, you have the power to thwart illegal collection efforts using your own script. Using your own script can help you remain calm and focused on your task; disputing invalid debts and controlling the ball.

It's extremely important to keep your wits about you during collection calls because collectors are trained to keep you off balance. Before responding, always **STOP** and **THINK**! Do not allow yourself to be drawn into a discussion, argument, or debate over the validity of any debt you suspect is not valid! **NEVER** discuss amounts, account numbers, previous payments or anything else. Stay focused! If you believe the debt to be invalid, then stand your ground and dispute the debt!

Collectors use leading questions and double talk to get you to admit to some minor detail like, when the last payment was made or the last time you used the account. Once you start discussing (and agreeing) with these minor details, you're on a slippery slope headed toward admitting the debt is valid when it may not be.

Experienced collectors are very good at getting you to agree a debt is valid before you realize what you've said! Even if you didn't agree the debt is valid, they'll twist your words around so much you'll start thinking maybe you did say it. Once that happens, you've given up control and opened yourself up to all kinds of abuse.

I highly recommend keeping copies of your script by your home and work phones, so you can refer to it when collection calls come in. If you remember nothing else when the call comes in, remember to dispute, dispute, and dispute.

When that call does come in, verbally dispute the debt, and insist the collector follow the FDCPA. Section 809(a) requires collectors to inform you of the amount of the debt and what proof they have of the debt's validity. They must also tell you that, unless you dispute the debt in writing within 30 days, they will assume the debt is valid. They only have to reveal the name of the original creditor if you ask, so always ask! If collectors do not provide this information during their initial contact, they are required to mail you the information within 5 business days.

Let me highlight two points here!

1. When you agree to debts being valid, collectors are under no legal obligation to send you a FDCPA collection notice or validation documents. So, always dispute debts you believe to be invalid and always request validation in accordance with the FDCPA!

2. If you verbally dispute a debt, collectors are required to send you a collection (dunning) letter that describes the debt in question and your rights, including how to dispute the debt. If you ask, they are also required to give you the name and address of their company, the company they represent, and the creditor they represent (if applicable).

Remember; as soon as you verbally dispute any debt, expect collectors to try to get you to admit the debt might be valid! Again, don't fall for this tactic! Stand your ground! Insist they follow the FDCPA and send you a collection letter, so you may properly investigate and dispute the debt.

Reputable collectors send the collection letter right out, and some even include copies of whatever proof they might have. Reputable collectors provide the information needed to properly dispute the debt, such as account number, amount of debt, creditor's name, and an address to which you can send your dispute letter. Some even provide a format for your dispute letter. These professional collectors have one goal mind; ensure they have the actual debtor, and if so, work with the debtor to resolve the issue and so do by staying within the bounds of the FDCPA.

On the other hand, there are collectors who go to great lengths to hide their information, especially their phone numbers. They refuse to give you any information because they want you to believe that you only have one choice; to pay! But, by now you know better.

So, what do you do when collectors refuse to give you their information? Use a simple yet very powerful technique; record the phone conversation. In fact, I highly recommend recording all collection calls.

Let's say you've verbally disputed a debt and asked the collector for his company name and address, what creditor he represents and for him to send you a collection letter, but he refuses. Follow this next part verbatim.

Interrupt him in mid-sentence and say, "Excuse me while I turn on my tape recorder." Ignore whatever he says and remain silent for about 30 seconds (time this because it's very powerful). Turn on your recorder and then say, "Alright Mr. (or Ms.) Collector, I am now recording this conversation. Please tell me your name, company name, the creditor you represent and describe the debt you claim I owe."

This technique throws many collectors so far off balance they just hang up on you. Don't get drawn into a debate over whether taping the call is necessary or even legal. (Even though in many states it is legal to record calls without the other person's permission, always tell the collector you are recording the call; it's a powerful message that lets you control the ball).

You do not owe the collector an explanation of why you're taping the call, but if he insists, state, "Because of your refusal to provide me the information I request, which is a flagrant violation of the FDCPA, I am duty bound to file a formal complaint against you and your company with my State Attorney General, the Federal Trade Commission and the Better Business Bureau."

If your phone system does not have a built in system for recording conversations, purchase an answering machine or buy an inexpensive digital recorder capable of recording several minutes of conversation. Another option is to use your phone's speaker option, and then use a regular or handheld tape recorder to tape the conversation.

Recording collection calls keeps collectors on their toes, and it lets you refer back to the conversation for information such as names, dates, amounts, addresses and especially evidence of FDCPA violations in case legal action becomes necessary. Reputable collectors don't mind being recorded because they stay within the boundaries of the FDCPA. By the way, this technique goes both ways, so be prepared for collectors to record conversations as well so remain polite and professional no matter what the collector does.

After verbally disputing the debt and requesting the collector send you a collection letter outlining the debt and your rights, mark your calendar so you'll know exactly when five days are up. Then, if you have not received anything from the collector and he calls again, switch on your recorder and tell him you are still waiting.

Your 30 days to dispute the debt begins the day you receive the dunning letter, not the date the letter was signed or mailed. As soon as you determine the debt is not valid, send the collector a written dispute letter. Always try to send this letter on the same day you receive the collection letter.

Why the rush? Keep in mind that collectors are NOT prohibited from pursuing you while waiting on your written dispute. This means they can call (and they will), and they can file for a court hearing (some do), so sending out the letter right away will stop all collection actions (except for those collectors who ignore your letter – more on that later).

> **Note: Section 809 of the FDCPA states that failure to respond within 30 days does not mean you admit liability for the debt. The FTC has also stated that if you do not respond within 30 days, you DO NOT forfeit your right to dispute the debt at any time in the future.**

Section 809: Validation of debts [15 USC 1692g] Item (c) "The failure of a consumer to dispute the validity of a debt under this section may not be construed by any court as an admission of liability by the consumer."

If you've been provided enough information over the phone to dispute the debt, (amount, original creditor, account number, interest and other fees and so forth) prepare your dispute letters but wait for collectors to send you the required dunning information according to the FDCPA. This gives you a paper trail that can offer protection down the road. Here is a sample <u>Initial Debt Dispute Letter</u> (pg. 90) for disputing invalid debts.

To sum up the initial collection call

Keep a copy of your collection script handy.

Always verbally dispute the debt. Stick to your dispute, regardless of any verbal judo the collector uses.

Do everything in writing. This is extremely important! Accurate records will save your bacon if you ever have to defend your position in court. I recommend using some type of folder or box for storing all documents related to the debt. Name the folder and put in bold letters, DO NOT DESTROY UNTIL 20XX (minimum of 15 years later).

Note: I've seen debt collection attempts on debts more than 14 years old, so keep the records for a minimum of 15 years; 21 years is even better.

Record all calls! As mentioned earlier, this is a powerful tool for keeping collectors on their toes and abiding by the FDCPA. Many collectors abandon their efforts when they know they're dealing with a savvy debtor.

Keep accurate records. This is just as important as doing everything in writing. Accurate means keeping track of the time and date of collection calls and the name(s) of callers, all collector correspondence including envelopes and copies of everything you send out, including mail receipts.

What happens after your Initial Dispute?

Usually one of the following scenarios…

Scenario #1: Collectors cease their collection efforts

This is the most common occurrence because collectors almost always lack enough documentation to validate the debt in court. The original creditor has more than likely destroyed any records pertaining to the debt; thus, collectors cannot validate the debt as required by the FDCPA. So, rather than waste time, effort, and money on problematic accounts, collectors cease their collection efforts and move on to greener pastures.

However, collectors rarely tell you they've abandoned their efforts. Instead, they sell the account to the next Junk Debt Buyer, and a month or two later a different collector contacts you. When this happens you must begin the dispute process again.

You're probably thinking, "But I thought collectors had to respond within 30 days?" The 30-day rule applies to debtors, not collectors. Many people mistakenly believe collectors have only 30 days to respond, but the FDCPA requires collectors to respond to your dispute only if they intend to pursue further collection actions!

809. Validation of debts   [15 USC 1692g]

(4) a statement that, if the consumer notifies the debt collector in writing within the 30-day period the debt, or any portion thereof, is disputed, the debt collector will obtain verification of the debt or a copy of a judgment against the consumer, and a copy of such verification or judgment will be mailed to the consumer by the debt collector; and

(5) a statement that, upon the consumer's written request within the 30-day period, the debt collector will provide the consumer with the name and address of the original creditor, if different from the current creditor.

(b) If the consumer notifies the debt collector in writing within the 30-day period described in subsection (a) that the debt, or any portion thereof, is disputed, or that the consumer requests the name and address of the original creditor, the debt collector shall cease collection of the debt, or any disputed portion thereof, until the debt collector obtains verification of the debt or any copy of a judgment, or the name and address of the original creditor, and a copy of such verification or judgment, or name and address of the original creditor, is mailed to the consumer by the debt collector.

So, if after receiving your dispute letter, collectors choose not to pursue you, they are not required to send you any documentation. On the other hand, collectors who have not received a written dispute from you can continue demanding payment and even take legal action during the 30-day period you have for disputing a debt. So, it's imperative you dispute debts in writing as soon as possible!

Scenario #2: Collectors attempt to validate the debt

Many reputable collectors follow the FDCPA and validate debts using proper procedures. This means they receive a dispute, obtain proper documentation from the original creditor, and then send copies of this documentation to the debtor. Receiving word back from original creditors may take several weeks to months, so don't be surprised if you don't hear anything for quite some time!

On the other hand, many collectors make weak attempts at validating debts. Although this is due to several reasons, the most common reason is a lack of good record keeping. Collectors often send locally-produced documentation that would not stand up in court, but they hope (even expect) debtors to accept it as validation.

What is validation or verification?

Simply put, proper validation of a debt depends on the specific nature of the dispute. At a minimum, the debt collector is required to confirm with the creditor that the amount being claimed is correct and that the person he is attempting to collect the debt from is the person who owes it. The most basic response to a validation/verification request would be for the collector to provide the name of the original creditor and some simple statement regarding the alleged amount owed.

Many believe collectors must provide an expansive amount of information and answer an exhaustive list of specific validation questions…this is JUST NOT True!

The following text is posted on the website of Attorney Andy Nelms from Montgomery, Alabama…

HOW TO BEAT A COLLECTION LAW SUIT: 4 STEPS TO SUCCESS

The United States Fourth Circuit Court of Appeals has opined that validation can be nothing more complicated than this: "Verification of a debt involves nothing more than the debt collector confirming in writing that the amount being demanded is what the creditor is claiming is owed; the debt collector is not required to keep detailed files of the alleged debt." See, Chaudhry v. Gallerizzo, 174 F.3d 394 (1999).

I highly encourage you to read attorney Nelms' article titled, How to beat a collection law suit: 4 steps to success at:

http://www.debt-n-credit-letters.com/beat-collection-lawsuit.html

Seek a judgment

This scenario is the most dangerous one. Reputable collectors validate debts and then, if the debtor fails to respond, seek a judgment. In seeking a judgment, reputable collectors follow all procedures including proper filing of the court paperwork and notifying debtors of the court date.

On the other hand, less than reputable collectors use underhanded tactics including filing in court while ensuring the debtors are not aware of court hearing. If you don't show in court collectors are often granted **default judgments** (pg. 59) so, when notified of a court hearing, always show up and defend yourself! Failure to show up almost always results in a default judgment against you!

Your actions now depend on which scenario occurs.

Scenario One

Let's assume scenario number one takes place, and you never hear from the collector again. The does not mean the debt goes away. Instead, it gets sold to another Junk Debt Buyer who contacts you and demands payment. If this happens, simply dispute the debt again. Except, this time add to your dispute letter a reference to previous disputes.

Unfortunately, this cycle could repeat itself several times because the FDCPA prohibits collectors from discussing or sharing information about you with third parties, and other collectors fall into this category. Therefore, the collector with whom you dispute a debt cannot tell the next collector anything about you, including the fact that you dispute the debt.

I believe Congress needs to amend the FDCPA to allow collectors to share this information, and this information only. But until that happens, be prepared to dispute the same debt more than once. Use these sample letters, **Initial Debt Dispute Letter** (pg. 90) and **Debt Dispute Letter – New Collector** (pg. 94)

Scenario Two

Collector validates debt? This second scenario generally only happens on fairly new debts. Older debts are hard to validate because of lost or destroyed records.

When collectors properly validate debts AND you agree the debt is valid, then you have to fall back on your possible actions listed under **How to Handle Valid Debts** (Pg. 28).

When collectors send documents that you do not believe validate the debt, send a "debt still in dispute" letter that explains why you believe the debt is still invalid and what you believe to be wrong with the validation documentation. Use this sample **Debt Still Invalid Letter** (Pg. 96)

Scenario Three:

The final scenario involves judgments. I'll assume the judgment is a default judgment because any other type of judgment would mean you attended the court hearing and participated in the proceedings, thus you are aware of the outcome.

Chapter 5

Default Judgments

Default judgments are only granted when the defendant (debtor) fails to appear in court. Reasons why debtors fail to appear in court include:

Choose not to appear for many reasons but mostly because they believe they can't win…nothing could be further from the truth;

Are unable to attend due to circumstances beyond their control; or

Are unaware of the court hearing (this happens way too often).

Let's begin by examining the decision not to appear. Perhaps debtors choose not to appear because they believe they have no chance of winning, or they think they need an attorney or they think the collector does not have a case.

Whatever the reason, failure to appear in court almost guarantees a default judgment because, after examining the paperwork and ensuring everything appears to be in order, judges have no real choice but to assume that because the debtor failed to respond the debt must be valid and therefore award a default judgment.

I cover default judgments in depth later, but for now, understand that most default judgments are awarded because the debtor fails to show up in court.

Later in this guide I discuss what to do if you **discover a default judgment** (pg. 56) against you, but for now, if you are aware of the court hearing, ALWAYS show up! Why? Because more often than not, collectors have little to no evidence to prove the debt is valid and unscrupulous collectors violate the FDCPA which gives you an edge. Just showing up and disputing a debt can often result in the case (not the debt) being dismissed, or at the very least rescheduled (giving you time to consider your options and get to know your rights better so you are prepared for the next court appearance).

When debtors are unable to attend due to circumstances beyond their control, it's very possible to have a default judgment overturned if debtors can prove their reason for not showing up was really beyond their control.

In the case of debtors who are aware of the hearing but do not appear, the judge will want to know if the court was notified. If not, the chances of overturning (set aside) the judgment are pretty slim. One exception, as stated earlier, is debtors who had every intention of attending the hearing, but were prevented from doing so because of something outside their control. Plausible excuses include major accidents, incapacitating hospitalization, death in the family and natural disasters or similar circumstances that can be proven.

The final reason default judgments are granted is because debtors are unaware of the hearing. This occurs because debtors are not notified! This happens for two reasons; the court notice was mailed to your last known address and for some reason you did not receive it or, and there is no other way to put it except to say that unscrupulous debt collectors find ways to make it appear like you were properly notified even though you were not.

Judges look for valid (legal) reasons to grant or deny judgments based on the facts presented. If the court paperwork appears to be in order and you do not show up to defend your position, judges will normally grant the default judgment.

If more debtors showed up and challenged collectors' documentation and their failure to follow the FDCPA many, many cases would be dismissed.

After obtaining default judgments, collectors usually pursue legal permission to seize your bank account funds and garnish your wages before you realize what happened. While you're still trying to figure out what to do, collectors have already collected some, if not all, of the debt by seizing the funds in your bank accounts. Getting some or all of the money back might be possible, if you have a case for overturning the judgment but it requires an attorney well versed in this type of issue and lots of time and money!

Because hiring an attorney may cost more than the debt itself, many debtors do not pursue the issue. Remember, collectors purchase debts for pennies on the dollar, so collecting any money above the court fees and debt itself is pure profit.

Default Judgments can be overturned (set aside)

To be successful in overturning a default judgment, you must prove that you were not given due process (not given a fair chance to defend yourself).

Get a copy of the judgment from the court that issued it and comb through it looking for any discrepancies. Pay special attention to how you were supposedly notified. Quite often you'll discover the paperwork contains mistakes. If it does, (and they almost always do) use it to petition the court for a rehearing. Go to the hearing prepared with evidence that you were not notified, and, had you been notified; you would have presented evidence disputing the debt as invalid.

Quite often, contesting the debt may be enough to overturn default judgments (or prevent one in the first place) because collectors seldom produce enough evidence to prove the debt is valid or follow the FDCPA rules. Examples of evidence include:

The debt is not yours;

The debt was previously paid;

You can prove that you disputed the debt in writing, with the collector who was granted the default judgment. In addition, you can also prove the collector never validated the debt thus you were denied the opportunity to resolve the issue in "good faith" and avoid court.

Note: When collectors fail to follow the FDCPA and the rules of the court, you have an excellent chance of proving you were denied due process.

Section 811 of the FDCPA allows "debt collectors to sue consumers for the purpose of obtaining court judgments for debts, but only in the judicial district where the consumer resides or signed the contract, except that an action to enforce a security interest in real property which secures the obligation must be brought where the property is located.

Note: I'm often asked to clarify the above statement concerning credit card debts. Quite often we sign (accept) credit card contracts in the state we live in, while the credit card company resides in another state. The natural question is, "In which state can collectors file a lawsuit?" The answer is the state in which you live.

Keep in mind that even after being awarded a judgment, bill collectors, creditors, and debt collectors must still figure out how to collect the debt from you...courts do not collect judgments!

Judgments can expire and most states require renewal after so many years (generally between 6 and 10 years). Failure to renew a judgment renders it unenforceable. Remember this point because collectors try to collect on expired judgments. Unless you check with the court, you'll never know if the judgment is still enforceable. The easiest way to verify a judgment is to check with the clerk of the court where the judgment was granted. You can usually do this online or by making a simple phone call to the clerk.

Chapter 6

Garnishments

There are two types of garnishments: wage and bank account. First, I'll discuss what happens when your bank account is garnished and what you can do about it. Then I'll cover wage garnishment.

Bank Account Garnishment

You just swiped your debit card at the register of your favorite grocery store, and it says, "Access denied!" You try it again, same results! You know you should have money in the bank because your paycheck was just deposited.

So why are you being denied access to your own account? You whip out your cell phone and call your bank. Their answer, "Your funds were frozen by court order that morning by a collector who obtained a judgment and court order to garnish your account!"

Unfortunately this happens more often than people realize, and by the way...the day it happened was not just any day...it was a specific day selected by a savvy collector! The collector monitored your bank account for weeks, even months, (or called your employer and asked when checks are deposited) watching your deposit and withdrawal patterns, waiting until he could seize the greatest amount of funds.

A garnishment order forces your bank to freeze the funds and deny you access to your own account. Although you must also be notified of the garnishment, collectors purposely wait until after serving your bank before serving you. This prevents you from withdrawing your funds before they can be frozen.

Bank account garnishments occur without warning and do a tremendous amount of damage because any outstanding checks you've written will bounce causing returned check fees, and your name can end up on a local or national list of "Bad Check Writers."

Bank account garnishments can be placed against single and joint accounts, and, unless you can prove the funds are exempt, all funds in the account up to the amount of the debt can be seized, regardless of which account holder deposited the funds.

You'll receive paperwork for a court hearing. Make sure you attend this hearing because the purpose is to decide what to do with your funds! At the hearing you'll be able to present evidence that proves why all or some of the funds should not be released to you. If the garnishment is the result of a default judgment, see the section on **overturning default judgments** (pg. 56).

In most states, the garnishment can only freeze funds already in your account at the time of service on the financial institution. During the time the garnishment is in effect, the financial institution cannot honor checks or other orders for the payment of money drawn against your account. This means any outstanding checks will bounce or be returned for NSF. The exception to this rule is if your account has more on deposit than the amount of the garnishment. In this case, the bank can honor checks up to the amount that will not reduce your funds below the amount of the garnishment. When the amount being garnished is paid, the freeze on your account must be terminated. By the way, many banks also charge you a fee for processing the garnishment order. I've seen this range from just a few dollars up to $175. Some possible exemptions (funds that must be released from garnishment) include:

Veterans Benefits

Child Support Payments

U.S. Government Pension

Unemployment Compensation

Supplemental Security Income (SSI)

Temporary Assistance for Needy Families

Certain funds in a joint or community account

Other public Assistance or Income allowed by State Law

Also, depending on the state, you may be able to exempt a certain amount of funds for cash. The amount is typically $100, but can range up to $500 if you or someone you're supporting has a documented medical condition that requires care and/or medication. In order to protect your right to claim these exemptions, you must, within a certain number of days from the date on the Writ of Garnishment (typically 30 days or less), deliver to the court clerk (and mail a copy to the plaintiff) the completed exemption Claim Form.

Let me be clear on one point here! Only the funds already in your account can be frozen and possibly seized. This means any funds deposited afterwards are usually safe. However, many states allow additional account garnishment actions but usually limit the number of times an account can be garnished to a certain number per year (typically no more than once in any six month period). This is especially important to know if you have regularly scheduled direct deposits such as paychecks, disability checks, and so forth. If you have outstanding checks, BEFORE depositing any additional money in your account check with your state attorney general to see if additional funds can be seized. Finally, don't forget to stop direct deposit of nonexempt funds!

Wage Garnishment

This type of garnishment can be referred to as Administrative and Judicial (court-ordered). Although there are differences between the two types, we don't need to split hairs over all the technical differences. In the end, they both accomplish the same thing; force the deduction of money from your paycheck to pay a debt. The most common garnishments are child support, alimony, money judgments, defaulted student loans, and taxes. See your state's wage garnishment amounts here:

http://www.small-claims-courts.com/Wage-Garnishment-Laws.html

There are many rumors and myths about wage garnishments, so let's clear up the most common ones:

Federal law limits the maximum amount that can be garnished by one or more garnishment orders to 25 percent of your disposable earnings for that week, or the amount by which disposable earnings for that week exceed 30 times the federal minimum hourly wage, whichever is less.

Here are the federal minimum wage standards

$6.55 per hour from July 24, 2008 to July 23, 2009; then

$7.25 per hour after July 24, 2009

IMPORTANT: In simple terms, "disposable income" is whatever money you have left after paying all required taxes and national insurances! Disposable income is after-tax income that is officially calculated as the difference between personal income and personal tax and non-tax payments. In general terms, personal tax and non-tax payments are about 15 percent of personal income, which makes disposable personal income about 85 percent of personal income.

IMPORTANT: In order for wages to be garnished, disposable earnings per week must exceed 30 times the federal minimum hourly wage or $196.50 ($6.55 x 30). Put another way, if you make $196.50 or less per week, your wages cannot be garnished. Let's look at a couple examples:

Example using minimum wage amount from pre-July 2009

Weekly Earnings	Disposable Income	25 Percent of Disposable Income:
$262 ($6.55 x 40 hours)	$222.70 ($262 x .85)	$55.67 ($222.70 x .25 = $55.67)
Total amount of one or more garnishments per week: *$55.67		

*Remember the total of all garnishments combined cannot exceed 25 percent of disposable income.

Example using a _higher_ wage

Weekly Income	Disposable Income	25 Percent of Disposable Income:
$360 ($9.00 x 40 hours)	$306 ($360 x .85)	$76.50 ($306 x .25 = $76.50)
Total amount of garnishment per week: *$76.50		

*Remember the total of all garnishments combined cannot exceed 25 percent of disposable income.

Minimum Wage Information

States with higher minimum wages:

Washington, Oregon, California, Nevada, Arizona, Colorado, Maine, Iowa, Missouri, Illinois, Michigan, Ohio, West Virginia, Pennsylvania, Vermont, New York, Massachusetts, Connecticut, Rhode Island, New Jersey, Delaware, Alaska, Virgin Islands, Hawaii, and Florida

States with lower minimum wages:

Arkansas, Georgia, Kansas, Minnesota, New Mexico, Wisconsin, and Wyoming

States with no minimum wage law:

Alabama, Louisiana, Mississippi, South Carolina, and Tennessee (in these states the federal minimum wage applies)

Visit the government's official site to learn more about wage laws…http://www.dol.gov/dol/topic/index.htm

There are four exceptions to the 25 percent rule

Child support or alimony orders;

Orders of any court of the United States having jurisdiction over cases under chapter 13 of title 11, Bankruptcy Code;

Delinquent state or federal taxes; and

Defaulted student loans (limited to 10 percent of disposable income)

The maximum amount that can be garnished for support of any person cannot exceed:

50 percent of disposable earnings for that week when the individual is supporting a spouse or dependent child; or

Up to 65 percent of disposable earnings for that week when an individual is not supporting a spouse or dependent child. Learn more here: http://www.student-loan-default.com/FAQ-Employers.html

The maximum amount that can be garnished for defaulted student loans is 10 percent of disposable income. Use this link to learn more about defaulted student loans and how to stop garnishment actions: http://www.student-loan-default.com

No court of the United States or any State court, and no State (or officer or agency thereof), may make, execute, or enforce any order or process in violation of this section. Basically this means your state cannot override the federal law and deduct more than the maximums or ignore a garnishment order. However, states can (and some do) limit the maximum amount of garnishments to less than the 25 percent limit. Some states limit the number of days a garnishment can last and a few states require an additional hearing and waiting period before a garnishment takes effect. Always check your state garnishment laws to be sure of the rules governing your particular situation. See my small claims courts site to learn more…

http://www.small-claims-courts.com/Wage-Garnishment-Laws.html

Warning! **It's possible to have a 10 percent student loan garnishment and a 15 percent money judgment garnishment at the same time because they equal the 25 percent federal limit when added together.**

A Final Note on Garnishment: Title III of the **Consumer Credit Protection Act (CCPA)** prohibits an employer from discharging an employee whose earnings have been subject to garnishment for any one debt, regardless of the number of levies made or proceedings brought to collect it.

We've covered a lot of ground discussing valid and invalid debts, how to handle the initial debt collection call, default judgments, bank account and wage garnishments. That covers the general information you'll need to begin the debt dispute process. In the next few sections we'll cover specific debt collection and credit issues.

Chapter 7

When Collectors Lie to Credit Reporting Agencies

One question I am asked over and over is, "Can collectors who have purchased debts report them to credit reporting agencies (CRA) as new debts?" The answer is, not legally! However, they do report old debts anyway, and credit reporting agencies seldom cross reference information provided by collectors with information provided by creditors. So, debts can end up being reported more than once on the same report. Unless you dispute these duplicate debts, they remain on your credit reports for up to seven years.

As of December 29, 1997, the credit reporting period runs from the date of delinquency, NOT the date the debt is reported to the CRA. Most debts are reported for 7 years, while other debts, such as bankruptcies, can be reported for 10 years. Some special category debts can be reported indefinitely.

> **Special Note: The law does not say CRAs must report bankruptcy up to the 7- or 10-year point, only that they can if they choose to.**

Collectors report inaccurate debt information to CRAs more than credit providers do. Why do they do this? To get your attention, of course! Many people are able to ignore collection calls and avoid other collection activities, but when it comes to their credit reports, they take action to protect their credit rating which in turn prevents them from paying higher interest rates on mortgages, big-ticket items, and of course credit cards.

Therefore, collectors know the quickest method for gaining your attention is to mess with your credit reports. Collectors, who have been unsuccessful in contacting you or in getting you to return their calls, will add negative information to your credit report and then sit back and wait for you to call them.

Collection agencies often assign their own internal account numbers to old debts and then report the debt as a new account. They also report the last activity date wrong! This is one of the most common tactics.

The last activity date is the date you last took action on the account not the date a collector contacted you or took action on the account. Although collectors are not prohibited from assigning internal account numbers to debt accounts, they are supposed to report accurate information, especially the original date of delinquency.

What normally happens is the debt is reported as a new debt and shows up on your report, and now your report reflects two separate delinquent accounts for the same debt. With millions of pieces of credit history being reporting every day, CRAs do not take the time to cross reference items to eliminate duplicate entries or to verify the accuracy of the information being reported…most information is entered into your credit reports exactly as it is received…mistakes and all.

Additionally, the FCRA requires anyone reporting information to a CRA to report it accurately. So, the CRAs don't worry too much about whether the data is accurate or not because, if it's not accurate, the blame falls on whoever reported it rather than the CRA.

So what can you do if you discover a collector has incorrectly reported a debt? Well, the Fair Credit Reporting Act says if you dispute an item with the agency that reported it, and your claim is true, the agency is legally bound to correct the information. However, don't hold your breath waiting for collectors to correct your information.

If collectors have been calling you, and you have disputed the debt, send a letter to the collection agency demanding they correct whatever information they reported. At the very minimum, any debt in dispute that's reported to a CRA must be reported as "in dispute." This helps a little when creditors review your report but again, expect to correct the information in your reports yourself. I've built an entire self-help site dedicated to walking you through the process of disputing items directly with CRAs.

http://www.fair-credit-reporting.com/Credit-Reports/dispute-procedures.html

Now that you understand the importance of keeping an eye on your credit reports, let's turn to another tactic used by collectors…suing in small claims court.

Chapter 8

Small Claims Court

It's becoming more and more common for collectors to use small claims courts to seek money judgments against debtors. The reason is small claims court judges are very busy, looking at a dozen or more cases (not all cases are collection suits) a day. They don't have a lot of time to spend on a case, so when debtors fail to appear, small claims court judges are more likely than traditional courts to grant a default judgment.

I cannot emphasize this point enough; "the key to having a collector's case dismissed is to show up and dispute the debt!" As stated earlier, the chances of collectors having solid evidence proving the debt is yours are slim. I've also built an entire self-help site dedicated to helping you understand the small claims court process: http://www.small-claims-courts.com

Court Appearances

I suspect many people fail to appear in court because they are afraid of the unknown. Appearing in court can be intimidating, so I've included the following tips to help you through the experience:

Dress right! First impressions can have a tremendously positive impact and greatly increase your credibility. Wear business attire, and if you're female, wear conservative make-up and conservative jewelry.

Go prepared! Don't just show up and hope for the best. Prepare what you want to say and how you want to say it. Write it down and practice it.

Regular Courts: If you have documents to support your case, you must file your documents with the court according to the specific rules of the court. Every court is different so check the court's website or ask the clerk of the court for instructions.

Small Claims Courts: Some courts require the same procedures as regular courts while others are a bit more informal. Put your supporting documents in a neat, orderly package for the judge. Place a cover sheet on the package that describes the contents and outlines in chronological order what happened. The key here is to get to the point; be succinct, thorough and stick to the facts.

Do your homework!   Know your rights, what laws apply, and, specifically, what section of the law applies to your situation. Also know the rules of the court; procedures, filing deadlines and so forth. If the debt has expired, be prepared to say so and to also give the legal reference that supports your position. Remember, you are NOT an attorney, so don't try to act like one. But, being prepared shows you are trying to resolve the issue, not to mention the amount of time and effort you save the judge.

Mind your manners! Use proper titles such as Judge, Your Honor, sir, and ma'am. When referring to the plaintiff (creditor or collector), use Mr., Mrs., or Ms. Use please, thank you, excuse me and other similar courtesies.

NEVER interrupt the judge! Wait until you are asked to speak before saying anything, and then, speak clearly – don't ramble. Also, don't interrupt the plaintiff, even if you know the plaintiff is telling bold-faced lies! Wait your turn. If you do not understand something, politely ask for clarification.

Answer the judge's question! Many people don't realize how often they fail to answer someone's question. Listen carefully to what the judge is asking and then answer the exact question – don't ramble or add information the judge did not ask for. Take a few minutes to put your thoughts together before speaking. Sometimes the judge only wants a yes or no answer, other time they may ask for "just the facts." Be prepared to give the facts of the case including times, dates, amounts, locations, and so forth. Write this information down and read it if you have to…this helps keep emotions out of it!

Remain professional at all times!   Don't use profanity, slang, acronyms, or other jargon. Don't call people names or slander them! Don't accuse anyone of anything unless you have proof to support your accusation.

Stick to the facts! Do not embellish anything. If something is not a fact but you believe it to be important to your case, be sure to say, "In my opinion…"

Check your emotions at the door! Not doing this can really land you in hot water. Don't allow yourself to become angry, especially with the judge. Angry people don't think clearly, so keep your emotions in check! Getting angry will not help your case.

Using the above tips will go a long way toward making your court appearance more productive and a great deal less stressful.

Chapter 9

Bad Checks

Dishonored checks tendered in payment for goods or services acquired or used primarily for personal, family, or household purposes are covered under the FDCPA. Underhanded collectors will try to convince you that they do not have to follow the FDCPA rules...don't believe them.

Treat collection calls and dunning notices for bounced checks the same as you would any other debt. First, determine if the check (debt) is valid, and if so, decide whether to pay it or not. If the debt is not valid, use the same dispute procedures outlined earlier.

The statute of limitations (SoL) for enforcing a debt, in this case, a returned check, usually runs from 1-3 years depending on the state in which you live. Always check your state's statute of limitations as some might be longer that 3 years.

> **WARNING!** The above information does not apply to fraudulent activity. Writing checks with the intent to defraud someone is a crime! Collectors often claim you can be "arrested" for writing bad checks, or that it's "under investigation by their criminal division." Although it's true you can be arrested for writing bad checks if your intent was to commit fraud, making a mistake in your checkbook or in balancing your bank statement is not "intent to commit fraud." Before a warrant for your arrest can be issued, the collector needs to prove that your intent was criminal. That is unlikely in most returned check cases; therefore, the threat of being arrested often violates the FDCPA because the threat cannot usually be carried out and/or the collector has no intention of carrying out the threat.

Chapter 10

What to do when collectors violate the FDCPA

Collectors violate the FDCPA every day and get away with it! Perhaps it's because people are afraid to fight back when they do not know their rights, or believe they don't have any rights.

As I've pointed out several times in this guide, you have rights! Even when you're in debt up to your eyeballs, you still have rights. One of your most important rights is freedom from harassment and abuse.

It's critical that you report every violation of the FDCPA to your state attorney general and to the Federal Trade Commission (FTC). Each year the FTC reports to Congress the number of FDCPA violations and other debt-related complaints they receive. Because not everyone reports violations, I believe the actual number of violations is much higher than reported to Congress and therefore the FDCPA remains the same rather then be amended to strengthen its protections.

Until we ban together and report every violation, debt collectors will continue to get away with using illegal tactics and abusive language to harass people. Reporting violators helps provide Congress the data it needs to strengthen the FDCPA. And, your complaint could be the one that finally gets an unethical collector off the streets.

Please, take action to record and report violations.

Chapter 11

Debt and Credit Protection Laws

Fair Debt Collection Practices Act (FDCPA)

This is a federal law outlining debtors' and collectors' rights. It contains 18 chapters that cover terms and definitions, third-party contact rules, illegal harassment, abusive and false and misleading tactics, unfair collection practices, debt validation, debt payments, where debt collectors have to file lawsuits, deceptive collection letters and forms and civil liability for violations of the FDCPA. See this site for an in-depth look:

http://www.fair-debt-collection.com/rules/fair-debt-collection-act.html

Fair Credit Reporting Act (FCRA)

This federal law outlines the rights of consumers concerning credit reporting. Its 24 chapters cover permissible purposes, legal information, investigative reports, and compliance procedures, disclosures to governmental agencies and consumers, civil liability, dispute procedures, public record information for employment purposes, obtaining information under false pretenses, unauthorized disclosures, reporting of overdue child support obligations, responsibilities of furnishers of information, and disclosures to FBI for counterintelligence purposes:

http://www.fair-credit-reporting.com/fair-credit-reporting-act/FCRA.html

Truth-in-Lending Act (TILA)

The Truth-in-Lending Act requires "meaningful disclosure of credit terms" and reflects a shift in emphasis from "let the buyer beware" to "let the seller disclose." It protects consumers against inaccurate and unfair credit billing and credit card practices, too! It covers truth-in-lending disclosure statements, violations, and 3-day cooling-off periods:

http://www.creditcardsed.com/credit_laws/truth-in-lending-act.html

Wage Garnishment Law (AWG)

The best way to prevent garnishment is to be proactive when dealing with creditors and debt collectors. Wage garnishment (except student loans) is only possible after obtaining a court-ordered judgment. The garnishment can take up to 25 percent of your disposable income. This federal law, from Title 15, Chapter 41, and Subchapter II, covers restriction on garnishments and discharge from employment, exemption for State-regulated garnishments, enforcement, effect on State laws and garnishment of Social Security and Disability Benefits. It does not describe how to stop garnishment!

http://www.small-claims-courts.com/Wage-Garnishment-Laws.html

State and Civil Codes

Each state has its own codes and statutes. Some states adopt federal law, while others established their own debt and credit laws. For instance, several states use the FDCPA, which does not provide protection against creditors collecting their own debts. Other states enacted their own version of the FDCPA, but included creditors so consumers have protection from overzealous creditors. State laws may or may not offer more protection than federal law, so always check.

http://www.debt-n-credit-letters.com/state-laws.html

Chapter 12

Letters and Scripts

The following sample letters are very effective, so don't be afraid to use them. Be sure to insert your information where needed and feel free to change, add or delete words, as needed, to fit your situation. If you find you need something different, please visit my free site **http://www.debt-n-credit-letters.com/** where you'll find additional free sample letters.

Debt Payment Offer/Agreement Letter

Today's Date

Your Name
Your Address

Attention: {name of collector}
Name of Debt Collection Agency
Address

RE: Your {letter dated} or {phone call on date} reference account #: {place account or reference number here}

Dear Mr. /Ms. {Collector's Name}

I am not disputing this debt; however, given my current financial situation, I am unable to pay the amount you request. My records indicate the total due on this account is $_____

I am able to make (monthly, weekly, every two weeks etc.) payments on this account, to your company, in the amount of $ _____. I promise to mail payments every {day of week, or date of month} until this account is paid in full.

If you accept my offer, I look forward to working with you, and you can expect my first payment just as soon as I receive your written confirmation that you accept this offer. If my financial situation improves and I am able to increase my payment, I will contact you immediately. If you refuse my offer, then in accordance with the Fair Debt Collection Practice Act, Section 805(c): Ceasing communication, I respectfully request that you do not contact me again except to:

Advise me that further efforts are being terminated;

Notify me that you may invoke specified remedies;

Notify me that you intend to invoke a specified remedy.

Thank you for understanding my situation.

Sincerely,

Signature here
Your Printed Name

Phone Script for Handling Debt Collection Calls

Learn what to say and how to say it! Learn how to handle debt collection calls from nasty bill collectors who demand answers to personal questions and payments on debts that may or may not be valid.

Debt collectors ask questions designed to gather just enough personal information about you and your financial assets so they can figure out how much you can afford to pay or how much they can pursue through court action.

Collectors have a job to do, and many of them perform this distasteful duty in a very professional manner. However, there are many unprofessional collectors who use unfair and illegal tactics to collect debts.

Debt collectors who act professionally usually do so because they received training on how to collect debts without violating the FDCPA. In order to stay focused on their collection efforts (and not violate the FDCPA), many collection agencies and independent bill collectors use a dunning (collection) script.

Knowing what a typical script looks like can help you prepare answers to debt collectors' questions ahead of time and, with your own script in hand, help you remain calm and focused while dealing with unprofessional collectors.

I've provided two sample scripts below, along with my opinion of how to handle each scenario (Names in italics are made up).

> **Note: I highly recommend recording all phone calls from debt collectors (and creditors). Always inform the collector at the beginning of the call that you are taping the call. If asked why, calmly say, "So that I have a copy of this call for my records." If your phone system does not have a way to record conversations, purchase one that does, or as a last resort, get a small handheld tape recorder and keep it handy.**

Debt Collection Script #1 – You believe the debt to be invalid

Collector: "Hello, is Bill there?" (Or is this Bill's wife)?

You: "Who is calling, please?" (Do not let the use of your first name throw you off guard; always confirm with whom you are speaking. Under the FDCPA, collectors must identify themselves and, only when asked, the company they represent).

Collector: "This is Mr. Collector from ABC collections, the collection agency representing Way Past Due on your outstanding balance of $3,700. I need to know if you are able to take care of this past-due bill at this time.

You: "Hold on while I turn on my tape recorder." (After turning on recorder, ask the caller to repeat his or her name, company, and reason for calling.) Then say, "I do not believe I owe this debt. Send me the information on this debt according to the Fair Debt Collection Practices Act so that I may review it."

> **Notes: Expect the collector to use questions or statements in an attempt to get you to admit the debt is yours. Do not answer these questions; stick to the answer outlined above and insist to the collector that he or she follow the FDCPA by sending you the proper information…remember stay focused.**

Their script tells them to ignore your response and press on with asking you a bunch of questions. By refusing to take the "bait," you frustrate their efforts because your answer is not on their script. At this point, many collectors are unsure of what to say or do next, so they resort to anger, name-calling, and threats. Remain calm and be sure your tape recorder is on!

Once you've verbally disputed a debt, there is only one legitimate question that you need to answer:

Collector: "Please verify your address."

You: Go ahead and provide your correct address.

You do NOT need to answer additional questions! If the collector insists on asking questions, politely terminate the call. Expect the collector to call right back. Turn on your recorder and answer the phone. Wait for the collector to stop yelling, politely remind the collector you are recording the call, and since you disputed this debt during the previous call, this call violates the FDCPA and forces you to report the violation to the State Attorney General." Then, terminate the call again…politely of course.

Debt Collection Script #2 – You believe the debt might be valid, but you're unsure

<u>**Collector**</u>: "Hello, is Bill there?" (Or is this Bill's wife)?

You: "Who is calling, please?" (Do not let the use of your first name throw you off guard; always confirm with whom you are speaking. Under the FDCPA, collectors must identify themselves and, if asked the company they represent).

<u>**Collector**</u>: "This is Mr. Collector from ABC collections, the collection agency representing Way Past Due on your outstanding balance of $3,700. I need to know if you are able to take care of this past-due bill at this time."

*<u>**You**</u>*: "Hold on while I turn on my tape recorder."

Take your time and THINK before saying anything. Is it possible the debt has expired? See statute of limitations (SoL). If the SoL has expired (or you're not sure), revert to scenario #1.

If the SoL has not expired, then ask,

*<u>**You**</u>*: "Are you collecting on behalf of a creditor, your employer, or yourself?" DO NOT answer other questions until the collector answers this question.

IMPORTANT: **If the debt is new, the collector is probably working for the creditor. If the debt is more than 1-2 years old, it's a good bet the debt was sold, and this collector (or his company) purchased it.**

If the collector owns the debt and you do NOT wish to deal with the collector (be sure your tape recorder is on beforehand) state:

*<u>**You**</u>*: "It is my policy not to deal with debt collectors who are not representing the creditor. I do not believe this debt is valid; please send me the required FDCPA notifications so that I may deal with this situation in accordance with the FDCPA."

Be prepared for any and all of the questions below and consider each question carefully before answering. Remember, you do NOT have to answer any questions. However, if you choose to answer questions, see the section below on which questions you should answer and which ones you should weigh heavily before giving a stranger your information.

If the collector owns the debt and you still wish to pay it, then you must decide on how much to pay. Just remember, Junk Debt Buyers purchase old debts for pennies on the dollar and you should never agree to pay a debt until it has been verified.

Questions you should answer:

Do I have your address right at (street), (city) and (state) and (zip code)?

Is this (or what is) your daytime phone _____?

Note: After answering this question, inform the caller that any future calls between (hours) and on (days) are inconvenient.

Where do you work?

What is the address and phone number of your employer.

Note: Collectors are allowed to call and verify employment with your employer BUT that is all! They are not allowed to discuss your information, nor are they entitled to any information about your income or any other personal information.

Questions you should consider carefully before answering:

Are you paid weekly or bi-weekly?

How much is your take-home pay?

Is your spouse working? (If so, where, how is he/she paid, amount per week, etc.)

Do you have other sources of income (child support, part-time work, in-home day care and so forth)?

Do you rent or own? How much per month? Is it current?

How much is your car payment? Is it current?

What are the make, model, and year of your car(s)?

Where do you bank? (Checking and savings, name of bank)

Do you have any bank loans? How much do you owe? Are they current?

Have you ever borrowed money from (parents, relatives, and friends) in the past? If so, how much, did you pay it back, when?)

Recognize that every question is designed to find out information that can be used against you! If you choose to answer any of the above questions, then expect the collector to make several suggestions on how you could pay off the debt. Typically, they will come back with, "If I could show you a way to pay this debt off, would you be willing to work with me?"

Unless they suggest a payment plan that you can afford, **DO NOT** agree to anything! They'll suggest borrowing from others, refinancing your home or car loan, or putting the debt on another credit card. Using these options means robbing Peter to pay Paul, and, more than likely, will just push you deeper in debt.

Consider your answer carefully!! Counter offer with a payment agreement of your own (only suggest what you can truly afford) and ask about credit reporting information. You want to keep it off your credit reports, so make this part of your payment agreement negotiation.

Collectors are trained to dun (collect or ask for payment) in the following priority…

Balance in full;

Settlement (preferably in one payment but accept more than one);

Payments over 3 or more months, usually not to exceed 6 months;

Good faith payment while you ask others for a loan (parents, friends, bank etc. (Don't forget, making payments, of any amount resets the SoL and opens the door for a lawsuit)

…and since they want the full amount as quick as possible, they will refuse just about anything you offer and try to force you to agree to their terms.

Unless you're extremely good at negotiating, never negotiate terms on the phone; you'll lose every time. Offer your terms once (maybe twice), and if they refuse to work with you, end the conversation!

WARNING!   Be absolutely certain the Statute of Limitations (SoL) has not expired before agreeing to anything, but especially before making a token payment! In many states, a token payment or a written agreement to pay resets the SoL clock!

Collection agencies, bill collectors, and junk debt buyers are trained to get payments in the following priority:

Auto Pay: involves withdrawals from your bank accounts via postdated checks, automatic electronic withdrawals, or similar methods.

Check or Bank Note via Priority Mail

Check or Bank Note via Certified Mail

NOTE: Although collectors will insist on you paying by their preferred method, there is no law compelling you to pay by any of these methods! You should pay by a method that does not reveal your primary bank account to the collector. The best method is to pay by bank draft (from a bank other than the one you use) and send it via official mail.

WARNING!   Never pay by postdated check or an automatic withdrawal process. I've seen it happen too many times where the check is cashed early or more funds are withdrawn than authorized! This causes even more problems with returned checks and overdrawn charges!

Once they have a payment agreement, collectors usually end the call by saying (remember collectors also record calls):

"Please repeat the arrangement to be sure I've documented it correctly."

"What guarantee can you give me that you'll send the payment?"

"For what reason would you not send the payment?"

Hopefully you have been taking good notes or, even better, tape recording the call (inform the caller at the beginning of the call that you are taping the call) so you can also keep accurate records of what actions were agreed upon.

CAUTION! Do NOT send any money until you have a signed payment agreement letter in your possession!

Unable to Pay Letter (Judgment Proof)

Today's Date

Your Name
Your Address

Collector's or Creditor's Name
Address

RE: Account {insert account name and/or number}

Dear Collector or Creditor,

I am writing in response to your (letter or phone call) dated {insert date}, (copy enclosed) about the above referenced account. I am unable to pay on this account due to {insert reason here i.e. unemployed, disability}. This is a {permanent or temporary} situation.

I also hope to save both of us a great deal of time, energy and expense by letting you know I have no attachable income and do not own any assets, such as a home, car or land; essentially I have no money and can prove it!

I do not believe I owe this debt (or the amount stated) and thereby place it in dispute I agree, or use this alternative text .

I agree that I owe this debt and promise to keep you apprised of my status and, if future conditions allow, begin (or resume) making payments. Thank you for your understanding in this matter.

Sincerely

Signature here
Your Printed Name

Offer to Settle a Debt Letter

Today's Date

Your Name
Home Address

Attention: {name of person who contacted you}
Name of Creditor (or Collection Agency)
Address

RE: Collection letter dated {date of letter here} or phone call on {date of call here} reference account #: {account or reference number}

Dear Mr./Ms. {Creditor's or Collector's Name},

Although I agree I am responsible for the above referenced account, I do not agree that I owe as much as you claim. Therefore, I am offering to settle this account for $_____.

On the day I receive written confirmation that you accept my offer as a final settlement of all outstanding charges and fees, I will forward payment.

(Or you can use this alternative text . . .

As soon as I receive written confirmation that you accept my offer, I will mail a payment that day in the amount of $ _____ and additional payments in the amount of $ _____ every _____ days until the amount specified above is paid in full.

You agree to cease all attempts now, and in the future, to collect this debt including attempts by third-party collectors or attorneys. You also agree not to sell this account to any third party.

 Upon final payment, you further agree to remove all negative information, that you or your company placed in my personal credit reports with any and all credit reporting bureaus or agencies located in the United States.

Sincerely,

Signature here
Your Printed Name
CC: Original creditor (if sending to collector)

Do Not Call or Contact Me Letter (cease and desist)

Today's Date

Your Name
Your Address

Collector's Name
Collector's Address

Mr. /Ms. Collector,

I am writing in response to your constant phone calls!

Section 805(c)—Ceasing collection calls and communication of The Fair Debt Collection Practices Act (FDCPA) requires debt collectors to cease calling after being notified in writing.

Therefore, I demand that you stop calling me at home, at work, on my cell phone or at any other location. In accordance with the FDCPA, now that you have received this "cease and desist" letter, you may only contact me again to inform me that you:

> Are terminating further collection efforts;

> May invoke specified remedies which are ordinarily invoked by you or your company;

> Intend to invoke a specified remedy.

Be advised that I am well aware of my rights! For instance, I know that any future contact by you or your company CANNOT include a demand for payment and that you have my location information, so calls made by you or your company to any third party concerning me violates section 805(b)2 of the FDCPA.

I am keeping accurate records of all correspondence, including tape recording all phone calls. If you continue harassing me, I will pursue legal actions under the FDCPA against you and against the company you represent.

Signature here
Your Printed Name

Debt Previously Paid Letter

Today's Date

Your Name
Home Address
Phone Number

Attention: {name of collector if known}
Name of Debt Collection Agency
Address

RE: Collection letter dated {date of letter here} or phone call on {date of call here} reference account #: {account or reference number}

Dear Mr. /Ms. {Collector's Name of name of Collection Agency},

This letter is to inform you that the account in question was paid in full on [insert date] with [insert name of creditor or collection agency]. I have enclosed copies of the proof of payment. (Include if you have it, but don't worry about it if you don't)

Now that you have been informed of this debt being previously satisfied, I expect you to terminate your collection efforts and remove this account, and all references to my personal information, from your records.

I do not expect to hear from you again regarding this matter; however, should you choose to ignore this notification, I will consider any contact not in accordance with the Fair Debt Collection Act, a serious violation of the law, and will immediately report your actions to my State Attorney General and to the Federal Trade Commission. I will also take any and all legal action necessary to protect myself. Be advised that I tape record all phone calls.

Signature here
Your Printed Name

CC original creditor (if necessary)

Debt Previously Settled Letter

Today's Date

Your Name
Home Address
Phone Number

Attention: {name of collector if known}
Name of Debt Collection Agency
Address

RE: Collection letter dated {date of letter here} or phone call on {date of call here} reference account #: {account or reference number}

Dear Mr. /Ms. {Collector's Name of name of Collection Agency},

This letter is to inform you that the account in question was settled on [insert date] with [insert name of creditor or collection agency]. I have enclosed copies of the settlement letter and proof of payment. Now that you have proof that this debt was previously satisfied and no longer collectable, I expect you to terminate your collection efforts and remove this account, and all references to my personal information, from your records.

I do not expect to hear from you again regarding this matter; however, should you choose to ignore this notification, I will consider any contact not in accordance with the Fair Debt Collection Act, a serious violation of the law, and will immediately report your actions to my State Attorney General and to the Federal Trade Commission. I will also take any and all legal action necessary to protect myself. Be advised that I tape record all phone calls.

Signature here
Your Printed Name

Notes:

CC original creditor (if necessary)

Expired Statute of Limitation Letter

Today's Date

Your Name
Your Address

Collector's Name
Collector's Address

RE: [insert account number or name of account or name of debt]:

Dear [insert collector's name or company name],

This letter is in response to your [letter dated xx-xx-2004] (copy enclosed) or [phone call on xx-xx-2004], concerning the collection of the above referenced [account or date].

I have checked with my State Attorney General and verified that the Statute of Limitations for enforcing the collection of this debt in (insert your state or the state in which the property resides) has expired. Be advised that I am well aware of my right to use the "expired statute of limitations" as my defense, should you decide to pursue this matter in court.

This letter is your official notification that I consider this matter closed. Additionally, I demand that you, or anyone affiliated with your company, stop contacting me regarding this or any other matter, except to advise me that your debt collection efforts are being terminated, or that you or the creditor are taking specific actions allowed by Fair Debt Collection Practices Act (FDCPA) or my state law.

Be advised that any contact other than allowed by law is considered harassment and can result in you being personally fined up to $1,000 per incident. I will consider any contact not in accordance with the Fair Debt Collection Act, a serious violation of the law and will immediately report your actions to my State Attorney General and to the Federal Trade Commission. I will also take any and all legal action necessary to protect myself. Be advised that I tape record all phone calls.

Signature here
Your Printed Name

This Page Intentionally Left Blank

Initial Debt Dispute Letter (for disputing invalid debts)

Today's Date

Your Name
Your Address

Collector's Name
Collector's Address

Dear {insert name of collector or company},

This letter is being sent to you in response to a notice sent to me on (insert date letter sent by collector). Be advised that this is not a refusal to pay, but a notice sent pursuant to the Fair Debt Collection Practices Act, 15 USC 1692(g) that your claim is disputed and validation is requested.

This is NOT a request for "verification" or proof of my mailing address, but a request for VALIDATION made pursuant to the above named title and section. I respectfully request that your offices provide me with competent evidence that I have any legal obligation to pay you.

Please provide me with the following: a simple accounting of the debt, the name and address of the original creditor, and the original account number. Also, please show me that you are licensed to collect in my state and provide me with your license numbers and your Registered Agent.

Be advised that I am fully aware of my rights under the Fair Debt Collection Practices Act and the Fair Credit Reporting Act. For instance, I know that:

> You cannot add interest or fees, except those allowed by the original contract and state law.

> You do not have to respond to this dispute, except to tell me that you intend either to cease your collection efforts or to pursue other legal means of collecting this debt.

> Should you pursue a judgment without validating this debt, I will inform the court of your failure to follow the FDCPA.

> Any attempt to collect this debt without validating it, violates the FDCPA. Be advised that I record all phone calls, keep all correspondence, and will

not hesitate to report violations to my State Attorney General, the Federal Trade Commission, and the Better Business Bureau.

I have disputed this debt; therefore, until validated, you know your information concerning this debt is inaccurate. Thus, if you have already reported this debt to any credit-reporting agency (CRA) or Credit Bureau (CB), then you must immediately inform them that this debt is in dispute. Reporting information you know to be inaccurate or failing to report information correctly violates the FCRA § 1681s-2.

If you do NOT own the rights to collect this debt, I ask you to immediately send a copy of this dispute letter to the original creditor to whom you say I owe money, so they are also aware of my dispute with this debt.

Finally, in accordance with section 805(c)—Ceasing Collections, of the Fair Debt Collection Act, unless you are contacting me to validate this debt, do not contact me about this or any other matter, except by official mail and then only to advise me that your debt collection efforts are being terminated or that you are taking specific actions allowed by law.

Your anticipated cooperation in this regard is greatly appreciated.

Signature here
Your Printed Name

Follow-up Debt Dispute Letter

Use this letter when collectors fail to respond to first letter

Today's Date

Your Name
Your Address

Collector's Name
Collector's Address

Dear Collector,

I am writing in response to your {letter or phone call}, dated {insert date of letter or phone call}, copy enclosed.

On {insert date of initial dispute letter} I sent you a letter explaining that I do not believe I owe what you say I owe, and, in accordance with the Fair Debt Collection Practices Act, Section 809, I requested that you provide me, in writing, with a simple accounting of the debt, the name and address of the original creditor, and the original account number. Also, please show me that you are licensed to collect in my state and provide me with your license numbers and your Registered Agent.

I also requested that, if you have reported me to any credit reporting agency, you inform them I have placed this debt in dispute and provide me with proof that you have done so. Furthermore, I asked that you immediately send a copy of that dispute letter to the company (creditor) whom you say I owe money so they are aware of my dispute with this debt.

As of the date of this letter I have not heard from you. For your convenience, I have included a copy of my previous letter and a copy of the mail receipt showing that you received my letter on {insert date from mail receipt}.

Since you have failed to respond, I assume you have been unable to validate the debt; therefore, I consider this matter closed. This letter is your official notification that I do not intend to correspond with you on this matter again unless you comply with my requests, the FDCPA and the FCRA.

I must remind you that any attempt to collect this debt without validating it violates the FDCPA. Furthermore, I am recording all phone calls and keeping all correspondence concerning this matter and will not hesitate to report violations to my State Attorney General, the Federal Trade Commission, and the national Better Business Bureau.

Signature here
Your Printed Name

This Page Intentionally Left Blank

Debt Dispute New Collector Letter

Used to dispute the same debt but with a different collector.

Today's Date

Your Name
Your Address

Collector's Name
Collector's Address

Dear {insert name of collector or company},

I am writing in response to your (letter or phone call) dated, {insert date} (copy enclosed) because I do not believe that I owe what you say I owe.

This is the (insert number) time I have disputed this debt. The first dispute was on May 5, 2006, with the creditor, and the second was on September 1, 2007, with XYZ Collections. Neither the creditor nor the collection agency responded to my dispute letters.

In accordance with the Fair Debt Collection Practices Act (FDCPA), Section 809—Validating Debts, I respectfully request that you provide me with a simple accounting of the debt, the name and address of the original creditor, and the original account number. Also, please show me that you are licensed to collect in my state and provide me with your license numbers and your Registered Agent.

Be advised that I am fully aware of my rights under the Fair Debt Collection Practices Act and the Fair Credit Reporting Act. For instance, I know that:

You cannot add interest or fees, except those allowed by the original contract and state law.

You do not have to respond to this dispute except to tell me that you intend either to cease your collection efforts or to pursue other legal means of collecting this debt.

Should you pursue a judgment without validating this debt, I will inform the judge of your failure to follow the FDCPA.

After receiving this letter, any attempt to collect this debt without validating it violates the FDCPA. Be advised that I intend to record all phone calls, keep all correspondence and will not hesitate to report violations to my State Attorney General, the Federal Trade Commission, and the Better Business Bureau.

I have disputed this debt; therefore, until validated, you know your information concerning this debt is inaccurate. Thus, if you have already reported this debt to any credit-reporting agency (CRA) or Credit Bureau (CB) then you must immediately inform them that this debt is in dispute. Reporting information that you know to be inaccurate or failing to report information correctly violates the FCRA § 1681s-2.

If you do NOT own the rights to collect this debt, I ask that you immediately send a copy of this dispute letter to the original creditor whom you say I owe money so they are also aware of my dispute with this debt.

Finally, in accordance with section 805(c)—Ceasing Collections, of the Fair Debt Collection Act, unless you are validating this debt, do not contact me about this or any other matter, except to advise me that your debt collection efforts are being terminated or that you are taking specific actions allowed by law.

Signature here
Your Printed Name

Debt Still Invalid Dispute Letter

Use this letter to dispute debts where collectors provide poor or ineffective validation.

Today's Date

Your Name
Your Address

Collector's Name
Collector's Address

Dear {insert name of collector or company},

I am writing in response to the debt you say I owe and the documentation you provided supposedly proving that I owe this debt. I do not consider your documentation valid for the following reason(s):

(Add your reasons here—here are a few examples)

You failed to provide me *(use all that apply)*

> With a simple accounting of the debt;

> The name and address of the original creditor and account number; and

> Proof that you are licensed to collect in my state and provide your license numbers and your Registered Agent; and

> Provide a verification or copy of any judgment (if applicable);

> The amount indicates fees and interest charges not allowed under state and federal law.

In my opinion, you have failed to properly validate this debt in accordance with the Fair Debt Collection Practices Act (FDCPA), Section 809—Validating Debts. Therefore, I consider this debt as "still in dispute," and any contact from you other than to provide documentation to clear up the reasons for my dispute as outlined above, violates the FDCPA.

I have already advised you in a previous letter that I am fully aware of my rights under the Fair Debt Collection Practices Act and the Fair Credit Reporting Act, and that I will not hesitate to take all legal steps necessary to protect myself.

Finally, in accordance with section 805(c)—Ceasing Collections, of the Fair Debt Collection Act, unless you are providing proper validation, do not contact me about this or any other matter, except by official mail and then only to advise me that your debt collection efforts are being terminated or that you are taking specific actions allowed by law.

Signature here
Your Printed Name

Mailing and Record Keeping Instructions

Step 1: Write the letter (initial or follow-up dispute, creditor's agreement, or free credit report request etc.). Consider handwriting your letter, but if you type it, be sure to sign it and send the original to avoid it looking like a form letter.

Step 2: Sign and date all letters in black ink!

Step 3: Make 2 copies of your signed letter and 2 copies of any attachments.

Step 4: Fax the letter and all attachments (keep the fax confirmation sheet for your records)

Step 5: Staple the original attachments to a copy of your letter, and save for your files.

Note: Send original letters, but never send original receipts or other original documents.

Step 6: Properly address two envelopes with the correct return address, but do not put stamps on them!

Step 7: Staple one set of attachment copies to your original letter, and place in envelope #1.

Step 8: Staple one set of attachment copies to a copy of your original letter, and place in envelope #2.

Note: Original letter refers to copies of the letter that you have signed.

Step 9: Take both letters to the Post Office and mail according to the following mailing instructions:

Envelope # 1

Send certified mail with return receipt requested, then take the cash receipt stamped with the amount and date, and, when your certified return receipt arrives via the mail, save both of these in a file marked "Credit Disputes."

Envelope #2

Send by first-class mail using a "certificate of mailing" (proof that it was mailed). Keep the dated/stamped cash receipt and ask for a dated/stamped "certificate of mailing" (small extra fee) receipt, then save both of these in a file marked "Credit Disputes."

Maintaining Proof of Your Mailing Actions

You should have the following items as proof for each letter you send:

A copy of the creditor, debt collector, or credit reporting agency letter;

The envelope that the documents in item number 1 above came in;

A copy of your signed letter with attachments stapled to it;

A fax confirmation sheet;

A dated/stamped cash receipt from the post office (envelope #1);

A return receipt, after it arrives in the mail (envelope #1);

A "certificate of mailing" receipt (envelope #2 -first-class letter);

A cash receipt for the "certificate of mailing" (envelope #2);

Place all of these in a folder marked "Credit Disputes" and file away in a safe place for at least 15 years.

I highly recommend that you check your current State's Statute of Limitations to see if you should keep the records longer than 15 years.

Chapter 13

Statute of Limitations

The Statute of Limitations is a time limit, set by each state, that is the legal amount of time creditors and collectors have to use the court system to enforce the collection of a debt.

The statute of limitations depends on the type of debt. Generally, unsecured debt expires between three and six years after the last missed payment or the consumer's last activity on the account. Written contracts, such as car loans, generally expire after six years. Judgments can last up to 21 years but usually require a renewal at the 6- to 10-year point.

> **WARNING!** **There is NO statute of limitations on federal student loans, most taxes and fines, and in many states, there is no time limit on past due child support. Some states have a SoL on income taxes whiles others do not.**

Generally, the statute of limitations for collecting debts begins either the moment you sign a credit contract or the moment you breach a contract depending on state law. For instance, you sign a contract on 1 June, to pay someone $500 on 10 December, of the same year. In some states the SoL begins on 1 June, the day you signed the contract, while in other states it begins on 11 December, the first day after the date you failed (breached) to pay the debt.

Every state has specific rules on the "running of a statutory period", and some states also have provisions to adjust or toll (stop) this period.

Many states use the term "toll" or "tolled" in their statute of limitations rules. Tolled means "stop the running of a statutory period for a certain period of time."

For example, let's say that you live in Florida where the statute of limitations on credit card debt (open ended credit) is four years. You do not make any payments to your credit card company for two years, leaving only two years to go before the statute of limitations for enforcing the collection of the debt expires. Suddenly, you move to Georgia, stay several months, and then move back to Florida.

Under Florida statutes, leaving the state tolls (stops) the running of the statutory period. So, on the day you move back to Florida, the remaining two-year statutory period begins running again.

On the other hand, if you had two years left on the statutory period and suddenly decided to make payments for 12 months but then stopped again, the four-year statutory period begins running again on the date you stopped making payments; in effect, you reset the SoL clock.

Making a payment, a promise to pay in writing or acknowledging in writing that the debt is valid can reset or restart the statute of limitations. This is especially true for credit cards, loan payments, and similar types of credit.

> **WARNING! While the statute of limitations (SoL) is running, or even after it's expired, making ANY payment or signing a promissory note can reset or restart (depends on your state law) the statute of limitations. Always check if the SoL has expired BEFORE making a payment, agreeing to make a payment, or signing an agreement to make payments!**

EXAMPLE: Let's assume the SoL on a personal loan in your state is four years. On January 1, 2000, you sign the loan papers with the first payment due February 1, but you never make a payment. The four-year SoL expires February 1, 2004, (four years from the date of the last payment due date on which no payment was made).

Using the above example, let's assume you receive a collection call in February 2003 (one year before the SoL expires), and, based on that call, you make a $50 payment with a promise to pay each month. That payment either tolls (stops) the collection time clock or resets it, depending on state law. If you fail to make another payment and your state allows the clock to be reset, then, in this example, the clock restarts from the date of the next missed payment and runs another four years.

Credit cards and personal loans are good examples of "stopping the collection time clock" because each monthly payment restarts the clock. These payments are usually minimum payments and are normally for unsecured credit (although unsecured has no effect on the SoL). Secured credit is usually not a collection issue because the creditor simply seizes (repossesses the item).

However, it's worth mentioning that, in most cases, items that are repossessed are often sold at auction for far below what is owed. The result is an unsecured debt that the debtor may still be responsible for paying and one that has a SoI.

The statute of limitations for the collection of debts is not well known and is often misunderstood. Many debt collectors are not aware of the statute of limitations or that each state has its own specific rules. Collectors who know about the SoL are hoping you do not know about it or, more importantly how to use it to protect yourself!

> **IMPORTANT! Many people, including debt collectors and creditors, believe the statute of limitations for credit reporting (7 to 10 years) is the same as the statute of limitations for collecting debts! They are not the same! For in-depth information about the SoL, see my site:** http://www.fair-credit-reporting.com/credit-laws/credit-reporting-periods.html

When collection agents call demanding payment on an old debt, and you make ANY payment, even a small "token payment," you may reset or restart the clock and open the door for collectors to seek a judgment against you. Judgments are state dependent but can run as long as 21 years. Most must be renewed to remain in effect beyond a certain period of time.

I've seen cases where collectors have called about debts for which the statute of limitations (time allotted to legally enforce a debt) expired 15 years earlier.

> **IMPORTANT: Although the SoL has expired, it's not illegal for collectors to attempt the collection of these debts.**

> **IMPORTANT: Debts discharged in bankruptcy are not collectable from the person who was granted the bankruptcy discharge. However, co-signers can still be pursued.**

Understand that collectors can still take you to court to try and enforce the collection of debts, but, if you raise the "Expired Statute of Limitations" defense and meet your state's qualifying criteria, the judge may dismiss the case.

If the statute of limitations has expired, send an **"Expired SoL Letter"** (pg. 88) that informs the collector you are aware of the expired SoL defense, and, if the collector pursues court collection efforts, you will use it as your defense. Most collectors realize pursing the case any further is a waste of time and resources and drop the case, but not always. Some hope you are bluffing and try anyway.

> **WARNING!** **You must raise the expired statute of limitations issue yourself! The judge cannot mention it, and the collector definitely won't bring it up, so you must do it. If you don't show up or mention the SoL, the collector stands a good chance of winning a default judgment against you.**

Even though the statute of limitations has expired, that does not mean you can't be hauled into court. That's why you must appear in court to raise the expired statute of limitations (SoL) defense. You can win, but YOU must be present in court AND you must be the one to bring up the expired SoL!

Just remember, winning a judgment gives collectors a long time to pursue you!!!

Collectors are very good at convincing you to make a "token" payment, as a show of "good faith on your part," to prove that you intend to honor your debt. They never mention the SoL and, after receiving your payment, quietly seek a judgment against you.

> **IMPORTANT NOTE: If you discover you're the victim of a default judgment, immediately get copies of the court papers and look for inaccurate information, especially an outdated address. Showing the collector used the wrong information to file the court petition, opens the possibility for a rehearing because the collector knew of your whereabouts but failed to provide the that information. It is possible to have judgments overturned (set aside) if you can prove that you were not given due process to defend yourself in court.**

Credit Reports

Do not confuse the statute of limitations for debt collection with the statute of limitations for credit reporting. See the rules here:

http://www.fair-credit-reporting.com/credit-laws/credit-reporting-periods.html#3

For example, let's say your State's statute of limitations for collecting credit card debt is only four years. After fours years, you can legally refuse to pay the debt; however, according to the Fair Credit Reporting Act (FCRA), the debt can still be reported for seven years from the date of your last missed payment date.

Collectors hope that; because the debt is still on the credit report, you'll think they can still collect and will usually threaten court action! Don't fall for this tactic—ALWAYS check the debt's Statute of Limitations BEFORE agreeing to any payment plan, before verbally acknowledging the debt is valid or, more importantly, making a payment!!

The federal FCRA limits credit reporting agencies or credit bureaus from reporting certain types of debt beyond 7 or 10 years, except for tax liens which remain for seven years AFTER being paid or indefinitely if not paid. If you make an offer to pay or settle a tax debt for a smaller amount, be advised that the statute of limitations for reporting the debt can be extended. There are other exceptions to these time limits, for more information please visit:

http://www.fair-credit-reporting.com

Credit Reporting Time Clock

The Fair Credit Reporting Act clearly defines how long negative information can be reported! Learn more at:

http://www.fair-credit-reporting.com/credit-laws/credit-reporting-periods.html

> IMPORTANT: **New activity by anyone other than you, especially debt collectors, DOES NOT restart the credit reporting time clock. Also, checking on your credit reports and/or correcting information in them will not reset the SoL clock.**

Statute of Limitations on Debts by State

Note: The information below is current as of this writing however; laws change all the time so always verify the information with your state attorney general.

Alabama Statutes of Limitations

Contracts under seal: 10 years, (A.C. 6-2-33)

Contracts not under seal; actions on account stated and for detention of personal property or conversion: 6 years (A.C. 6-2-34)

Sale of goods under the UCC: 4 years (A.C. 7 -2- 725)

Open accounts: 3 years (A.C. 6-2-37)

Actions to recover charges by a common carrier and negligence actions; 2 years, (A.C. 6-2-38)

Actions based on fraud: 2 years (A.C. 6-2-3)

Alaska Statutes of Limitations

Action on a sealed instrument: 10 years (A.S. 09.10.40)

Action to recover real property: 10 years (A.S. 09.10.30)

Action upon written contract: 3 years (A.S. 09.10.55)

Note: prior to 8/7/97 -the statute of limitations for written contracts was 6 years.

Action upon contract for sale: 4 years (A.S. 45.02.725); however, limitations by agreements may be reduced, but not less than 1 year (A.S. 45.02.725).

Arizona Statutes of Limitation

Written contracts: 6 years, runs from date creditor could have sued account.

Oral debts, stated or open accounts: 3 years.

Actions for fraud or mistake: 3 years from the date of the discovery of the fraud or mistake.

Actions involving fiduciary bonds, out of state instruments and foreign judgments: 4 years.

NOTE: Arizona applies its own statute of limitations to foreign judgments rather than that of the state that originally rendered the judgment whether the judgment is being domesticated under the Uniform Enforcement of Foreign Judgments Act or pursuant to a separate action on the foreign judgment.

An Arizona judgment must be renewed within 5 years of the date of the judgment.

Arkansas Statutes of Limitations

Written contracts: 5 years,

NOTE: Partial payment or written acknowledgement of default stops this statute of limitations. (A.C.A. 16-56-111)

Contracts not in writing: 3 years, (A.C.A. 16- 56-105)

Breach of any contract for the sale of goods covered by the UCC: 4 years, (A.C.A. 4-2- 725)

Medical debts: 2 years from date services were performed or provided or from the date of the most recent partial payment for the services, whichever is later. (A.C.A. §16-56-106)

Negligence actions: 3 years after the cause of action. (A.C.A. § 16-56-105)

California Statutes of Limitation

Written agreements: 4 years, calculated from the date of breach.

Oral agreements: 2 years.

The statute of limitation is stopped only if the debtor makes a payment on the account after the expiration of the applicable limitations period.

Colorado Statutes of Limitation

Domestic and foreign judgments: 6 years and renewable each 6 years.

Note: If for child support, maintenance or arrears the judgment (lien) stays in effect for the life the judgment without the necessity of renewal every 6 years.

All contract actions, including personal contracts and actions under the UCC: 3 years (C.R.S. 13-80-101), except as otherwise provided in 13-80-103.5; All claims under the Uniform Consumer Credit Code, except sections 5-5-201(5): All actions to recover, detain or convert goods or chattels, except as otherwise provided in section 13 -80-103.5.

Liquidated debt and un-liquidated determinable amount of money due; Enforcement of instrument securing the payment of or evidencing any debt;

Action to recover the possession of secured personal property; Arrears of rent: 6 years, (C.R.S. 13-80-103.5)

Connecticut Statutes of Limitation

Written contact, or on a simple or implied contract: 6 years, (CGS 52-576)

Oral contract, including any agreement wherein the party being charged has not signed a note or memorandum: 3 years, (CGS § 52-581)

Delaware Statutes of Limitation

General contracts: 3 years;

Sales under the UCC: 4 years

Notes 6 years;

Miscellaneous documents under seal: No limitation.

District of Columbia Statutes of Limitation

Contract, open account or credit card account: 3 years from the date of last payment or last charge. NOTE: An oral promise to pay restarts the 3 years.

Contracts under seal: 12 years.

UCC Sales of Goods: 4 years.

Florida Statutes of Limitation

Contract or written instrument and for mortgage foreclosure: 5 years. F.S. 95.11.

Libel, slander, or unpaid wages: 2 years.

Judgments: 20 years total, and to be a lien on any real property, it has to be re-recorded for a second time at 10 years.

The limitations period begins from the date the last element of the cause of action occurred, (95.051). NOTE: The limitation period is tolled (stopped) for any period during which the debtor is absent from the state and each time a voluntary payment is made on a debt arising from a written instrument.

Almost all other actions fall under the 4-year catchall limitations period, (F.S. 95.11(3)(p)).

Georgia Statutes of Limitation

Breach of any contract for sale: 4 years, (OCGA 11-2- 725) NOTE: Parties may reduce limitation to not less than 1 year, but not extend it. A cause of action accrues when the breach occurs, regardless of the aggrieved party's lack of knowledge of the breach.

Contract, including breach of warranty or indemnity: 4 years, (OCGA 11- 22A-506) NOTE: The parties may reduce the period to 1 year.

Written contract: 6 years from when it becomes due and payable and the 6-year period runs from the date of last payment. (OCGA 9-3-24)

Open account: implied promise or undertaking: 4 years, (OCGA 9-3-25). NOTE: Payment, unaccompanied by a document acknowledging the debt, does not stop the statute. Therefore, the statutory period runs from the date of default, not the date of last payment.

Bonds or other instruments under seal, 20 years, (OCGA 9-3-23)

NOTE: No instrument is considered under seal unless it's stated in the body of the instrument.

Hawaii Statutes of Limitation

Breach of contract for sale under the UCC: 4 years.

Contract, obligation, or liability: 6 years.

Judgments: 10 years, renewable if an extension is sought during the 10 years.

NOTE: The time limitation stopped during the time of a person's absence from the state or during the time that an action is stayed by injunction of any court.

Idaho Statutes of Limitation

Breach of contract for sale under the UCC: 4 years.

Written contract or liability: 5 years

Contract or liability that is not written: 4 years. NOTE: The time period begins as of the date of the last item, typically a payment or a charge under a credit card agreement. A written acknowledgement or new promise signed by the debtor is sufficient evidence to cause the relevant statute of limitations to begin running anew. Any payment of principal or interest is equivalent to a new promise in writing to pay the residue of the debt.

Judgments: 5 years but may be renewed for another 5-year period.

NOTE: An independent action on a judgment of any court of the United States must be brought within 6 years.

The time limitation for the commencement of any action is tolled during the time of a person's absence from the state or during the time that an action is stayed by injunction or by statutory prohibition action.

Illinois Statutes of Limitation

Breach of contract for sale under the UCC: 4 years.

Open account or unwritten contract: 5 years.

NOTE: Except, as provided in 810 ILCS 5/2- 725 (UCC), actions based on a written contract must be filed within 10 years, but if a payment or new written promise to pay is made during the 10-year period, then the action may be commenced within 10 years after the date of the payment or promise to pay.

Domestic judgments: 20 years, but can be renewed during that 20-year period.

Foreign judgments are the same time as allowed by the laws of the foreign jurisdiction.

Tolling: A person's absence from the state or the time that an action is stayed by injunction, court order or by statutory prohibition tolls the time limit.

Non-Sufficient Funds (NSF or Payment of Negotiable Instruments) checks: 3 years of the dishonor of the draft or 10 years after the date of the draft, whichever expired first: 810 ILCS 5/3-118.

Indiana Statutes of Limitation

Breach of contract for sale under UCC: 4 years.

Unwritten accounts or contracts and promissory notes or written contracts for payment of money executed after August 31, 1982: 6 years.

Written contracts unrelated to the payment of money: 10 years.

Written acknowledgement or new promise signed by the debtor, or any voluntary payment on a debt, is sufficient evidence to cause the relevant statute of limitations to begin running anew.

Judgments: 10 years unless renewed.

Iowa Statutes of Limitation

Open account: 5 years from last charge, payment, or admission of debt in writing. Unwritten contracts: 5 years from breach.

Written contracts: 10 years from breach

Demand note: 10 years from date of note.

Judgments: 20 years. However, an action brought on a judgment after 9 years, but not more than 10 years, can be brought to renew the judgment.

NOTE: Deficiency judgments on most residential foreclosures and judgments on mortgage notes become essentially worthless 2 years from date of judgment.

Kansas Statutes of Limitation

Written agreement, contract, or promise: 5 years

Expressed or implied but not written contracts, obligations, or liabilities: 3 years.

Relief on the grounds of fraud: 2 years.

Kentucky Statutes of Limitation

Recovery of real property: 15 years (KRS 413.0 10).

Judgment, contract, or bond: 15 years (KRS 413.110).

Breach of sales contract: 4 years (KRS 355.2- 725).

Contract not in writing: 5 years (KRS413.120). NOTE: Action for liability created by statute when there is no time fixed by statute: 5 years (KRS413.120).

Action on check, draft, or bill of exchange: 5 years (KRS 413.120).

Action for fraud or mistake: 5 years (KRS 413.120).

Actions not provided for by statute: 10 years (KRS 413.160).

Louisiana Statutes of Limitation

Contracts: 10 years.

Open accounts: 3 years.

Lawsuits which are filed but not pursued become null 3 years after the last action taken.

Judgment: 10 years, and if not renewed within the 10 years becomes a nullity.

Maine Statutes of Limitation

Generally all civil actions must be commenced within 6 years after the cause of action accrues. (14 M.R.S.A. 752).

The primary exception is for liabilities under seal, promissory notes signed in the presence of an attesting witness, or on the bills, notes or other evidences of debt issued by a bank, in which case, the limitation is 20 years after the cause of action accrues. (14 M.R.S.A. 751).

Judgments are presumed paid after 20 years. (14 M.R.S.A. 864).

Maryland Statutes of Limitation

Civil action: 3 years from the date it accrues, unless:

Breach of contract under any sale of goods and services under the UCC: 4 years after the cause of action, even if the aggrieved party is unaware of the breach.

Promissory notes or instruments under seal, bonds, judgments, recognizance, contracts under seal, or other specialties: 12 years.

Financing statement: 12 years, unless a continuation statement is filed by a secured party 6 months prior to end of 12-year period. (Maryland, Commercial Law article Sec. 2-725; Courts & Judicial Proceedings Article Sec. 5-101-02, 9-403).

NOTE: The 3-year statute of limitations begins again if creditors can document that a debtor has reaffirmed a debt by a good faith basis by a written agreement, orally, or by payment.

Massachusetts Statutes of Limitation

Debt instruments issued by banks, Contract under seal: 20 years.

Judgments: 20 years.

Oral or Written Contracts: 6 years.

Consumer Protection Actions: 4 years.

Recovery of Property: 3 years.

Probate Claims: 1 year from date of death.

Claims on mortgage notes following foreclosure or on claims junior to a foreclosed mortgage: 2 years.

Michigan Statutes of Limitation

Breach of Contract: 6 years, (MCL 600.5807(8).

Breach of Contract for Sale of goods under the UCC: 4 years, including deficiency actions following repossession and sale of goods subject to a security interest, (MCL 440.2725(1).

Judgments: 10 years, but are renewable by action for another 10 years, MCL.600.5809(3).

NOTE: Another state's limitation period may apply; check statutes carefully.

Minnesota Statutes of Limitation

Breach of contract for sale under the UCC: 4 years, (MSA 336.2.).

NOTE: Except where the Uniform Commercial Code otherwise prescribes, actions based on a contract or other obligation, express or implied, must be brought within 6 years after the cause of action occurred (Chapter 541).

Tolling: New written acknowledgement or payment tolls the statute of limitations for the debt.

Judgments: 10 years.

Mississippi Statutes of Limitation

Contracts and Promissory Notes: 3 years (MCA 75-3-118, 75-2-725, and 15-1-49).

Open Accounts: 3 years from the date at which time the items on the account became due and payable, (MCA 15-1-29 & MCA 15-1-31).

Judgment liens on real estate: 7 years, but can be renewed by filing suit to renew judgment prior to expiration of 7th year, (MCA 15-1-47).

Deficiency claims: 1 year from sale of collateral, (MCA 15-1-23).

Enforcement of construction liens: 1 year from date lien is filed, (MCA 85- 7-141).

Missouri Statutes of Limitation

Written agreement that contemplates the payment of money or property: 10 years, (Mo.Rev. Stat. §516.ll 0). NOTE: Under certain circumstances, the contractual statute of limitations may be reduced to 5 years.

Open accounts: 5 years, (Mo. Rev. Stat. §516.120).

Sale of goods under the UCC: 4 years.

NOTE: The statute begins to run from the date when the breach occurred for contracts and from the time of the last item in the account on the debtor's side for actions on accounts.

Montana Statutes of Limitation (MCA Title 27, Chapter 2)

Written contract, obligation, or liability: 8 years

Contract, account, or promise that is not based on a written instrument: 5 years.

Montana obligation to provide a certain level of support for a spouse, child, or indigent parent: 2 years.

Obligation or liability, other than a contract, account, or promise not based on a written instrument: 3 years.

Relief on the grounds of fraud or mistake: 2 years.

Judgment or decree of any U.S. court: 10 years. NOTE: Judgments rendered in a court not of record: 6 years.

NOTE: A written acknowledgement signed by the debtor or any payment on a debt is sufficient evidence to cause the relevant statute of limitations to begin running anew.

Nebraska Statutes of Limitation

Real estate or foreclosure mortgage actions; product liability; 10 years

Foreign judgments, contract or promise in writing, express or implied: 5 years.

Unwritten contract, express or implied; Recovery of personal property; Relief on grounds of fraud; breach of contract for sale of goods; and open account: 4 years.

Liability created by federal statute with no other limitation: 3 years. Malpractice: 2 years.

NOTE: SoL can be interrupted by partial payment or written acknowledgement of debt. The statute starts to run anew from the date of the partial payment or written acknowledgement, (Neb. Rev. Stat. §25-216).

NOTE: Actions on breach of contract for sale may be reduced to not less than 1 year.

Nevada Statutes of limitation

Written contract: 6 years

Verbal contract: 4 years.

Property damage: 3 years.

Personal injury: 2 years.

New Hampshire Statutes of Limitation

Contracts and open accounts: 3 years, (RSA 508:4).

Contracts for the sale of goods under UCC: 4 years, (RSA 382-A: 2-725).

Notes, defined as negotiable instruments: 6 years (RSA 382-A: 3-118).

Judgments, recognizance, and contracts under seal: 20 years (RSA 508:5).

Notes secured by a mortgage: 20 years and applies even if the mortgage has been foreclosed, (RSA 508:6).

Tolling: Payment on an account tolls the statute.

NOTE: Installment loans allow for separate measurement of the statutory period as each separate payment comes due, unless the loan has been accelerated.

New Jersey Statutes of Limitation

Conversion of an instrument for money: 3 years, (N.J.S.A.12A: 3-118(g)).

Sale of goods under the UCC: 4 years, (N.J.S.A. 12A; 2-725).

Real or personal property damage, recovery and contracts not under seal: 6 years (N.J.S.A. 2A: 14-1).

Demand Notes when no demand is made: 10 years. If demand made: 6 years from date of demand, (12A: 3-118(b)).

Obligations under seal for the payment of money only, except bank, merchant, finance company or other financial institution: 16 years, (N.J.S.A. 2A: 14-4) actions for unpaid rent if lease agreement is under seal, (N.J.S.A. 2A: 14-4).

Real estate: 20 years, (N.J.S.A. 2A: 14-7); Judgments: 20 years, renewable, (2A: 14-5); Foreign judgments: 20 years (unless period in originating jurisdiction is less), (2A: 14- 5).

Unaccepted drafts: 3 years from date of dishonor or 10 years from date of draft, whichever expires first, (12A: 3- 118(c)).

New Mexico Statutes of Limitation

Contract in writing: 6 years (except any contract for the sale of personal property is 4 years or the last payment, whichever is later).

All other creditor-debtor transactions are 4 years after accrual of the right to sue.

Judgments: 14 years.

NOTE 1: An action accrues on the first date on which the creditor can sue for a breach or for relief, generally from the last purchase or the last payment.

NOTE 2: If the limitations period has expired, an acknowledgment or payment starts the period running again.

New York Statutes of Limitation

N. Y. Civil Practice Law and Rules: Chapter Eight of the Consolidated Laws, Article 2—Limitations of Time:

211. Actions to be commenced within 20 years. (a) On a bond. (b) On a money judgment. (c) By state for real property. (d) By grantee of state for real property. (e) For support, alimony or maintenance.

212. Actions to be commenced within 10 years. (a) Possession necessary to recover real property. (b) Annulment of letters patent. (c) To redeem from a mortgage.

213. Actions to be commenced within 6 years: where not otherwise provided for; on contract; on sealed instrument; on bond or note, and mortgage upon real property; by state based on misappropriation of public property; based on mistake; by corporation against director, officer, or stockholder; based on fraud.

213-a. Actions to be commenced within 4 years; residential rent overcharge.

213-b. Action by a victim of a criminal offense.

214. Actions to be commenced within 3 years: for non-payment of money collected on execution; for penalty created by statute; to recover chattel; for injury to property; for personal injury; for malpractice other than medical or dental malpractice; to annul a marriage on the ground of fraud.

UCC, Section 2--725. Statute of Limitations in Contracts for Sale. (1) An action for breach of any contract for sale must be commenced within 4 years after the cause of action has accrued. By the original agreement, the parties may reduce the period of limitation to not less than 1 year but may not extend it. (2) A cause of action accrues when the breach occurs, regardless of the aggrieved party's lack of knowledge of the breach. Contract for lease of goods: 4 years (N. Y. U.C.C. 2-A-506(1).

S 203. Method of computing periods of limitation generally. (a) Accrual of cause of action and interposition of claim. The time, within which an action must be commenced, except as otherwise expressly prescribed, shall be computed from the time the cause of action accrued to the time the claim is interposed.

North Carolina Statute of Limitation

Express or implied contract, not under seal: 3 years.

Contract and sale of personal property under seal: 10 years.

Open account: 3 years, NOTE: Each payment renews the SoL on all items purchased within the 3 years prior to that payment. If no payment is made, the SoL runs from date of each individual charge. Contracts: From date of breach or default, unless waived or performance under the contract is continued.

Judgments: 10 years

Partial payment BEFORE the SoL expires renews the SoL from date of payment.

Payment AFTER SoL expires renews SoL ONLY if, at time of payment, circumstances infer the debtor recognized obligation to pay. Partial payment on open account restarts SoL on purchases made within 3 years of payment date; if acknowledgment can be inferred, starts the statute anew as to the full obligation acknowledged, even if all of the charges were not made within the last 3 years.

Partial payment by one debtor does not renew the statute of limitations as against any a co-debtor unless that co-debtor agreed to, authorized or ratified the partial payment.

Partial payments DO NOT affect the 10-year limitation on enforcing or renewing judgments.

Bankruptcy, Death or Disability: Filing of a bankruptcy tolls the statute of limitations for the enforcement of contracts and judgments.

The death, minority, disability, or incompetence of a debtor also tolls the limitation period until such time as a personal representative of the estate or a guardian of the incompetent or minor is appointed.

North Dakota Statutes of Limitation

Breach of contract for sale under the UCC: 4 years.

All other actions based on a contract, obligation, or liability, express or implied: 6 years.

NOTE: A new written acknowledgement or promise or voluntary payment on a debt revives the statute of limitations for the debt.

Judgments: 10 years.

Ohio Statutes of Limitation

Written or oral account: 6 years, (O.R.C. §2305.07).

Written contract: 15 years, (O.R.C. §2305.06).

Oral contract: 6 years (O.R.C. §2305.07).

Note payable at a definite time: 6 years, (O.R.C. § 1303 .16(A)); (2)).

Demand note: 6 years after the date on which demand is made or 10 years if no demand is made and neither principal nor interest has been paid over that time (O.R.C. §1303.16(B)).

Dishonored check or draft: 3 years after dishonor, (O.R.C. §1303.16 (C)).

Oklahoma Statutes of Limitation

Written Contract: 5 years, (O.S. § 95(1)).

Oral Contract: 3 years, (O.S. § 95(2)).

Attachments: 5 years, (O.S. § 95(5)).

Domestic Judgment: 5 years, (O.S. § 95(5)).

Foreign Judgment: 3 years, (O.S. § 95(2).

Oregon Statutes of Limitation

Unlawful trade practices: 1 year, (ORS 646.638(5).

NOTE: There is no statute of limitations for a cause of action brought as a counterclaim to an action by the seller. (ORS 646.638(6)).

Contract or liability: 6 years, (ORS 12.080).

Judgment: 10 years, (ORS 12.070).

Pennsylvania Statute of Limitations

Contracts: 4 years, (used to be 6).

Contracts under seal: 20 years.

Sale of goods under UCC: 4 years.

Negotiable instruments: 6 years (13 PA C.S.A. .§3118).

Rhode Island Statutes of Limitation

Contracts and open accounts: 10 years (9-1-13(a)).

Breach of a sales agreement under the UCC: 4 years, (6A-2- 725(1)).

Contracts or liabilities under seal and judgments: 20 years, (9-1-17).

Hospital liens: 1 year from payment, (9-3-6).

Against insurer to enforce repairer's lien: 1 year from payment to insured, (9-3-11).

Support obligations of common-law father: 6 years, (15-8-4).

Mechanic's lien: notice given is 1 year and 120 days, (34-28-10. 10).

South Carolina Statutes of Limitation

Breach of Contract: 3 years, (SCCLA 15-3-530).

NOTE: A partial payment or acknowledgment in writing tolls the SoL, (SCCLA 15-3-30).

Foreign or Domestic Judgments: 10 years, (SCCLA 15-3-600).

South Dakota Statutes of Limitation

Contract: 6 years, (SDCL 15-2-13).

Domestic Judgments: 20 years, (SDCL 15-2-6).

Foreign Judgments: 10 years, (SDCL 15-2-8).

Claims of Fraud: 6 years, (SDCL 15-2-13).

Sealed Instrument: (except real estate): 20 years, (SDCL 15-2-6).

Actions not otherwise provided for: 10 years, (SDCL 15-2-8).

Open Accounts: 6 years, (SDCL 15-2-13).

Sale of Goods: 4 years, (SDCL57A-2-725).

Tennessee Statute of Limitation

Breach of contract: 6 years, (T. C.A. 28-3-109).

Open accounts: 6 years, (T. C.A. 28-3-109).

Domestic or foreign judgments: 10 years, (T.C.A. 28-3-110).

Texas Statutes of Limitation

The Texas Civil Practice & Remedies Code provides a 4-year limitations period for all types of debt. The SoL begins after the day the cause of action accrues, (Section 16.004 (a) (3)).

Utah Statutes of Limitation

Any signed, written contract, obligation or liability: 6 years.

Unwritten contract, obligation, or liability: 4 years.

Open account for goods, wares, merchandise, and services rendered or for the price of any article charged on a store account: 4 years.

Judgment or decree of any court or State of the United States: 8 years.

NOTE: A written acknowledgement signed by the debtor revives the SoL.

Virginia Statutes of Limitation

Open account: 3 years from the last payment or last charge for goods or services rendered on the account.

Written contracts (non-UCC): 5 years.

Sale of goods under the UCC: 4 years.

Virginia Judgments: 10 years, and renewable (extended) to 20 years.

Foreign judgments: 10 years.

Vermont Statutes of Limitation

Contracts and goods on account: 6 years.

Witnessed promissory notes: 14 years

Washington Statutes of Limitation

Written contracts and accounts receivable: 6 years, (RCW 4.16.040).

Oral contract: 3 years (RCW 4.16.080).

Recovery of property and judgments: 10 years, (RCW 4.16.020).

West Virginia Statutes of Limitation

Unwritten and implied contracts: 5 years, (W. Va. Code 55-2-6 (1923)).

Breach of a sale of goods, lease of goods, negotiable instruments and secured transactions under the UCC, is found Article 46 of the West Virginia Code.

NOTE: If a debtor makes an acknowledgment by a new promise, or voluntarily makes a partial payment on a debt, under circumstances that warrant a clear inference that the debtor recognizes the whole debt, the statute of limitations is revived and begins to run from the date of the new promise, (W. Va. Code §55 -2-8)

Wisconsin Statutes of Limitation

Contracts, professional services, or an open account based on a contract: 6 years.

NOTE: Payments made toward the obligation toll the statute, and the time period will then run from the date of last payment or last charge by the debtor, whichever occurs later.

Wyoming Statutes of Limitation

Any contract, agreement or promise in writing: 10 years, (WS 1-3-105(a) (i)).

Unwritten contract, express or implied: 8 years, (WS 1-3-105(a)(ii)).

Recovery of personal property: 4 years, (WS 1-3-1 05 (a) (iv)).

Dishonor of draft (check): 3 years, (WS 34.1-3-118(c)).

Judgment: 21 years.

NOTE 1: Judgments cannot be revived after 21 years unless the party entitled to bring the action was a minor or subject to any other legal disability at the time the judgment became dormant; in this case action may be

brought within 15 years after disability ceases, (WS 1-16-503).

NOTE 2: If no execution is issued within 5 years from date of judgment or last execution is issued, the judgment becomes dormant and ceases to operate as a lien on the estate of the debtor, (WS 1-17-307).

NOTE 3: A dormant judgment may be revived in the same manner as prescribed for reviving actions before judgment or by action, (WS 1-16-502).

Ontario Statutes of Limitation

Since most debt actions are based in contract: 6 years from the date the cause of action arose (date of last payment or written acknowledgment of the debt). NOTE: If the contract provides that the law of another jurisdiction governs it, the limitation period of that jurisdiction will apply.

The post-judgment enforcement remedy of filing a writ of seizure and sale provides that the writ is valid for 6 years from the date it is issued, subject to renewal, which is the responsibility of the creditor. A discretionary procedure exists to renew an expired writ.

Actions on foreign judgments, including those from the United States, must be commenced within 20 years from the date of the foreign judgment. The merits of the defenses, if any, which were raised in the foreign debt action, are generally not available as defenses to the action on the judgment.

Virgin Islands Statutes of Limitation

Civil action under a contract or liability, express or implied: 3 years.

Instruments under seal, judgments, or decree of any court of the United States or of any state, commonwealth, or territory within the United States: 20 Years, (Title 5, Section 31, Virgin Islands Code).

Chapter 14

Definition of Creditors, Debt, and Debt Collector

Creditor

Section 803(4) defines "creditor" as "any person who offers or extends credit creating a debt or to whom a debt is owed." However, the definition excludes a party who "receives an assignment or transfer of a debt in default solely for the purpose of facilitating collection of such debt for another."

General: The definition includes the party that actually extended credit or became the obligee on an account in the normal course of business, and excludes [53 Fed. Reg. 50102] a party that was assigned a delinquent debt only for collection purposes.

Debt

Section 803(5) defines "debt" as a consumer's ". . . obligation to pay money arising out of a transaction in which the money, property, insurance, or services (being purchased) are primarily for personal, family, or household purposes ..."

The term includes:

Overdue obligations, such as medical bills, that was originally payable in full within a certain time period (e.g. 30 days).

A dishonored check that was tendered in payment for goods or services acquired or used primarily for personal, family, or household purposes.

A student loan, because the consumer is purchasing "services" (education) for personal use.

The term does not include:

Unpaid taxes, fines, alimony, or tort claims, because they are not debts incurred from a "transaction (involving purchase of) property . . . or services . . . for personal, family, or household purposes."

A credit card that a cardholder retains after the card issuer has demanded its return. The cardholder's account balance is the debt.

131

A non-pecuniary obligation of the consumer such as the responsibility to maintain adequate insurance on the collateral, because it does not involve an "obligation to pay money."

Debt Collector

Section 803(6) defines "debt collector" as a party "who uses any instrumentality of interstate commerce or the mails in any business, the principal purpose of which is the collection of any debts, or who regularly collects or attempts to collect, directly or indirectly, debts owed or due another."

Notwithstanding the exclusion provided by clause (F) of the last sentence of this paragraph, the term includes any creditor who, in the process of collecting his own debts, uses any name other than his own which would indicate that a third person is collecting or attempting to collect such debts.

For the purpose of section 808(6), such term also includes any person who uses any instrumentality of interstate commerce or the mails in any business the principal purpose of which is the enforcement of security interests.

The term includes:

Employees of a debt collection business, including a corporation, partnership, or other entity whose business is the collection of debts owed another.

A firm that regularly collects overdue rent on behalf of real estate owners, or periodic assessments on behalf of condominium associations, because it "regularly collects . . . debts owed or due another."

A party based in the United States who collects debts owed by consumers residing outside the United States, because he "uses . . . the mails" in the collection business. The residence of the debtor is irrelevant.

A firm that collects debts in its own name for a creditor solely by mechanical techniques, such as (1) placing phone calls with pre-recorded messages and recording consumer responses, or (2) making computer-generated mailings.

An attorney or law firm whose efforts to collect consumer debts on behalf of its clients regularly include activities traditionally associated with debt collection, such as sending demand letters (dunning notices) or making collection telephone calls to the consumer. However, an attorney is not considered to be a debt collector simply because he responds to an inquiry from the consumer following the filing of a lawsuit.

The term does not include:

Any person who collects debts (or attempts to do so) only in isolated instances, because the definition includes only those who "regularly" collect debts.

A credit card issuer that collects its cardholder's account, even when the account is based upon purchases from participating merchants, because the issuer is collecting its own debts, not those "owed or due another."

An attorney whose practice is limited to legal activities (e.g., the filing and prosecution of lawsuits to reduce debts to judgment).

Chapter 15

The Fair Debt Collection Practices Act

To amend the Consumer Credit Protection Act and to prohibit abusive practices by debt collectors, be it enacted by the Senate and House of Representatives of the United States of America in Congress assembled, That the Consumer Credit Protection Act (15 U.S.C. 1601 et seq.) is amended by adding at the end thereof the following new title:

801. Short Title [15 USC 1601 note]

This title may be cited as the "Fair Debt Collection Practices Act."

802. Congressional findings and declarations of purpose [15 USC 1692]

(a) There is abundant evidence of the use of abusive, deceptive, and unfair debt collection practices by many debt collectors. Abusive debt collection practices contribute to the number of personal bankruptcies, to marital instability, to the loss of jobs, and to invasions of individual privacy.

(b) Existing laws and procedures for redressing these injuries are inadequate to protect consumers.

(c) Means other than misrepresentation or other abusive debt collection practices are available for the effective collection of debts.

(d) Abusive debt collection practices are carried on to a substantial extent in interstate commerce and through means and instrumentalities of such commerce.   Even where abusive debt collection practices are purely intrastate in character, they nevertheless directly affect interstate commerce.

(e) It is the purpose of this title to eliminate abusive debt collection practices by debt collectors, to insure that those debt collectors who refrain from using abusive debt collection practices are not competitively disadvantaged, and to promote consistent State action to protect consumers against debt collection abuses.

803. Definitions [15 USC 1692a]

As used in this title --

(1) The term "Commission" means the Federal Trade Commission.

(2) The term "communication" means the conveying of information regarding a debt directly or indirectly to any person through any medium.

(3) The term "consumer" means any natural person obligated or allegedly obligated to pay any debt.

(4) The term "creditor" means any person who offers or extends credit creating a debt or to whom a debt is owed, but such term does not include any person to the extent that he receives an assignment or transfer of a debt in default solely for the purpose of facilitating collection of such debt for another.

(5) The term "debt" means any obligation or alleged obligation of a consumer to pay money arising out of a transaction in which the money, property, insurance or services which are the subject of the transaction are primarily for personal, family, or household purposes, whether or not such obligation has been reduced to judgment.

(6) The term "debt collector" means any person who uses any instrumentality of interstate commerce or the mails in any business the principal purpose of which is the collection of any debts, or who regularly collects or attempts to collect, directly or indirectly, debts owed or due or asserted to be owed or due another. Notwithstanding the exclusion provided by clause (F) of the last sentence of this paragraph, the term includes any creditor who, in the process of collecting his own debts, uses any name other than his own which would indicate that a third person is collecting or attempting to collect such debts. For the purpose of section 808(6), such term also includes any person who uses any instrumentality of interstate commerce or the mails in any business the principal purpose of which is the enforcement of security interests.

The term does not include --

(A) any officer or employee of a creditor while, in the name of the creditor, collecting debts for such creditor;

(B) any person while acting as a debt collector for another person, both of whom are related by common ownership or affiliated by corporate control, if the person acting as a debt collector does so only for persons to whom it is so related or affiliated and if the principal business of such person is not the collection of debts;

(C) any officer or employee of the United States or any State to the extent that collecting or attempting to collect any debt is in the performance of his official duties;

(D) any person while serving or attempting to serve legal process on any other person in connection with the judicial enforcement of any debt;

(E) any nonprofit organization which, at the request of consumers, performs bona fide consumer credit counseling and assists consumers in the liquidation of their debts by receiving payments from such consumers and distributing such amounts to creditors; and

(F) any person collecting or attempting to collect any debt owed or due or asserted to be owed or due another to the extent such activity (i) is incidental to a bona fide fiduciary obligation or a bona fide escrow arrangement; (ii) concerns a debt which was originated by such person; (iii) concerns a debt which was not in default at the time it was obtained by such person; or (iv) concerns a debt obtained by such person as a secured party in a commercial credit transaction involving the creditor.

(7) The term "location information" means a consumer's place of abode and his telephone number at such place, or his place of employment.

(8) The term "State" means any state, territory, or possession of the United States, the District of Columbia, the Commonwealth of Puerto Rico, or any political subdivision of any of the foregoing.

804. Acquisition of location information [15 USC 1692b]

Any debt collector communicating with any person other than the consumer for the purpose of acquiring location information about the consumer shall --

(1) identify himself, state that he is confirming or correcting location information concerning the consumer, and, only if expressly requested, identify his employer;

(2) not state that such consumer owes any debt;

(3) not communicate with any such person more than once, unless requested to do so by such person or unless the debt collector reasonably believes that the earlier response of such person is erroneous or incomplete and that such person now has correct or complete location information;

(4) not communicate by post card;

(5) not use any language or symbol on any envelope or in the contents of any communication effected by the mails or telegram that indicates that the debt collector is in the debt collection business or that the communication relates to the collection of a debt; and

(6) after the debt collector knows the consumer is represented by an attorney with regard to the subject debt and has knowledge of, or can readily ascertain, such attorney's name and address, not communicate with any person other than that attorney, unless the attorney fails to respond within a reasonable period of time to the communication from the debt collector.

805. Communication in connection with debt collection [15 USC 1692c]

(a)   COMMUNICATION   WITH   THE   CONSUMER GENERALLY. Without the prior consent of the consumer given directly to the debt collector or the express permission of a court of competent jurisdiction, a debt collector may not communicate with a consumer in connection with the collection of any debt --

(1) at any unusual time or place or a time or place known or which should be known to be inconvenient to the consumer. In the absence of knowledge of circumstances to the contrary, a debt collector shall assume that the convenient time for communicating with a consumer is after 8 o'clock ante meridiem and before 9 o'clock post meridiem, local time, at the consumer's location;

(2) if the debt collector knows the consumer is represented by an attorney with respect to such debt and has knowledge of, or can readily ascertain, such attorney's name and address, unless the attorney fails to respond within a reasonable period of time to a communication from the debt collector or unless the attorney consents to direct communication with the consumer; or

(3) at the consumer's place of employment if the debt collector knows or has reason to know that the consumer's employer prohibits the consumer from receiving such communication.

(b) COMMUNICATION WITH THIRD PARTIES. Except as provided in section 804, without the prior consent of the consumer given directly to the debt collector, or the express permission of a court of competent jurisdiction, or as reasonably necessary to effectuate a post-judgment judicial remedy, a debt collector may not communicate, in connection with the collection of any debt, with any person other than a consumer, his attorney, a consumer reporting agency if otherwise permitted by law, the creditor, the attorney of the creditor, or the attorney of the debt collector.

(c) CEASING COMMUNICATION. If a consumer notifies a debt collector in writing that the consumer refuses to pay a debt or that the consumer wishes the debt collector to cease further communication with the consumer, the debt collector shall not communicate further with the consumer with respect to such debt, except --

(1) to advise the consumer that the debt collector's further efforts are being terminated;

(2) to notify the consumer that the debt collector or creditor may invoke specified remedies which are ordinarily invoked by such debt collector or creditor; or

(3) where applicable, to notify the consumer that the debt collector or creditor intends to invoke a specified remedy.

If such notice from the consumer is made by mail, notification shall be complete upon receipt.

(d) For the purpose of this section, the term "consumer" includes the consumer's spouse, parent (if the consumer is a minor), guardian, executor, or administrator.

806. Harassment or abuse [15 USC 1692d]

A debt collector may not engage in any conduct the natural consequence of which is to harass, oppress, or abuse any person in connection with the collection of a debt. Without limiting the general application of the foregoing, the following conduct is a violation of this section:

(1) The use or threat of use of violence or other criminal means to harm the physical person, reputation, or property of any person.

(2) The use of obscene or profane language or language the natural consequence of which is to abuse the hearer or reader.

(3) The publication of a list of consumers who allegedly refuse to pay debts, except to a consumer reporting agency or to persons meeting the requirements of section 603(f) or 604(3) of this Act.

(4) The advertisement for sale of any debt to coerce payment of the debt.

(5) Causing a telephone to ring or engaging any person in telephone conversation repeatedly or continuously with intent to annoy, abuse, or harass any person at the called number.

(6) Except as provided in section 804, the placement of telephone calls without meaningful disclosure of the caller's identity.

807. False or misleading representations [15 USC 1962e]

A debt collector may not use any false, deceptive, or misleading representation or means in connection with the collection of any debt. Without limiting the general application of the foregoing, the following conduct is a violation of this section:

(1) The false representation or implication that the debt collector is vouched for, bonded by, or affiliated with the United States or any State, including the use of any badge, uniform, or facsimile thereof.

(2) The false representation of --

(A) the character, amount, or legal status of any debt; or

(B) any services rendered or compensation which may be lawfully received by any debt collector for the collection of a debt.

(3) The false representation or implication that any individual is an attorney or that any communication is from an attorney.

(4) The representation or implication that nonpayment of any debt will result in the arrest or imprisonment of any person or the seizure, garnishment, attachment, or sale of any property or wages of any person unless such action is lawful and the debt collector or creditor intends to take such action.

(5) The threat to take any action that cannot legally be taken or that is not intended to be taken.

(6) The false representation or implication that a sale, referral, or other transfer of any interest in a debt shall cause the consumer to --

(A) lose any claim or defense to payment of the debt; or

(B) become subject to any practice prohibited by this title.

(7) The false representation or implication that the consumer committed any crime or other conduct in order to disgrace the consumer.

(8) Communicating or threatening to communicate to any person credit information which is known, or which should be known to be false, including the failure to communicate that a disputed debt is disputed.

(9) The use or distribution of any written communication which simulates or is falsely represented to be a document authorized, issued, or approved by any court, official, or agency of the United States or any State, or which creates a false impression as to its source, authorization, or approval.

(10) The use of any false representation or deceptive means to collect or attempt to collect any debt or to obtain information concerning a consumer.

(11) The failure to disclose in the initial written communication with the consumer and, in addition, if the initial communication with the consumer is oral, in that initial oral communication, that the debt collector is attempting to collect a debt and that any information obtained will be used for that purpose, and the failure to disclose in subsequent communications that the communication is from a debt collector, except that this paragraph shall not apply to a formal pleading made in connection with a legal action.

(12) The false representation, or implication, that accounts have been turned over to innocent purchasers for value.

(13) The false representation, or implication, that documents are legal process.

(14) The use of any business, company, or organization name other than the true name of the debt collector's business, company, or organization.

(15) The false representation, or implication, that documents are not legal process forms or do not require action by the consumer.

(16) The false representation, or implication, that a debt collector operates or is employed by a consumer reporting agency as defined by section 603(f) of this Act.

808. Unfair practices [15 USC 1692f]

A debt collector may not use unfair or unconscionable means to collect or attempt to collect any debt. Without limiting the general application of the foregoing, the following conduct is a violation of this section:

(1) The collection of any amount (including any interest, fee, charge, or expense incidental to the principal obligation) unless such amount is expressly authorized by the agreement creating the debt or permitted by law.

(2) The acceptance by a debt collector from any person of a check or other payment instrument postdated by more than five days, unless such person is notified in writing of the debt collector's intent to deposit such check or instrument not more than 10 nor less than three business days prior to such deposit.

(3) The solicitation by a debt collector of any postdated check or other postdated payment instrument for the purpose of threatening or instituting criminal prosecution.

(4) Depositing or threatening to deposit any postdated check or other postdated payment instrument prior to the date on such check or instrument.

(5) Causing charges to be made to any person for communications by concealment of the true propose of the communication. Such charges include, but are not limited to, collect telephone calls, and telegram fees.

(6) Taking or threatening to take any nonjudicial action to effect dispossession or disablement of property if --

(A) there is no present right to possession of the property claimed as collateral through an enforceable security interest;

(B) there is no present intention to take possession of the property; or

(C) the property is exempt by law from such dispossession or disablement.

(7) Communicating with a consumer regarding a debt by post card.

(8) Using any language or symbol, other than the debt collector's address, on any envelope when communicating with a consumer by use of the mails or by telegram, except that a debt collector may use his business name if such name does not indicate that he is in the debt collection business.

809. Validation of debts   [15 USC 1692g]

(a) Within five days after the initial communication with a consumer in connection with the collection of any debt, a debt collector shall, unless the following information is contained in the initial communication or the consumer has paid the debt, send the consumer a written notice containing --

(1) the amount of the debt;

(2) the name of the creditor to whom the debt is owed;

(3) a statement that unless the consumer, within 30 days after receipt of the notice, disputes the validity of the debt, or any portion thereof, the debt will be assumed to be valid by the debt collector;

(4) a statement that if the consumer notifies the debt collector in writing within the 30-day period that the debt, or any portion thereof, is disputed, the debt collector will obtain verification of the debt or a copy of a judgment against the consumer and a copy of such verification or judgment will be mailed to the consumer by the debt collector; and

(5) a statement that, upon the consumer's written request within the 30-day period, the debt collector will provide the consumer with the name and address of the original creditor, if different from the current creditor.

(b) If the consumer notifies the debt collector in writing within the 30-day period described in subsection (a) that the debt, or any portion thereof, is disputed, or that the consumer requests the name and address of the original creditor, the debt collector shall cease collection of the debt, or any disputed portion thereof, until the debt collector obtains verification of the debt or any copy of a judgment, or the name and address of the original creditor, and a copy of such verification or judgment, or name and address of the original creditor, is mailed to the consumer by the debt collector.

(c) The failure of a consumer to dispute the validity of a debt under this section may not be construed by any court as an admission of liability by the consumer.

810. Multiple debts [15 USC 1692h]

If any consumer owes multiple debts and makes any single payment to any debt collector with respect to such debts, such debt collector may not apply such payment to any debt that is disputed by the consumer and, where applicable, shall apply such payment in accordance with the consumer's directions.

811. Legal actions by debt collectors   [15 USC 1692i]

(a) Any debt collector who brings any legal action on a debt against any consumer shall --

> (1) in the case of an action to enforce an interest in real property securing the consumer's obligation, bring such action only in a judicial district or similar legal entity in which such real property is located; or

> (2) in the case of an action not described in paragraph (1), bring such action only in the judicial district or similar legal entity --

>> (A) in which such consumer signed the contract sued upon; or

>> (B) in which such consumer resides at the commencement of the action.

(b) Nothing in this title shall be construed to authorize the bringing of legal actions by debt collectors.

812. Furnishing certain deceptive forms [15 USC 1692j]

(a) It is unlawful to design, compile, and furnish any form knowing that such form would be used to create the false belief in a consumer that a person other than the creditor of such consumer is participating in the collection of or in an attempt to collect a debt such consumer allegedly owes such creditor, when in fact such person is not so participating.

(b) Any person who violates this section shall be liable to the same extent and in the same manner as a debt collector is liable under section 813 for failure to comply with a provision of this title.

813. Civil liability [15 USC 1692k]

(a) Except as otherwise provided by this section, any debt collector who fails to comply with any provision of this title with respect to any person is liable to such person in an amount equal to the sum of --

> (1) any actual damage sustained by such person as a result of such failure;

> > (A) in the case of any action by an individual, such additional damages as the court may allow, but not exceeding $1,000; or

> > (B) in the case of a class action, (i) such amount for each named plaintiff as could be recovered under subparagraph (A), and (ii) such amount as the court may allow for all other class members, without regard to a minimum individual recovery, not to exceed the lesser of $500,000 or 1 per centum of the net worth of the debt collector; and

> (3) in the case of any successful action to enforce the foregoing liability, the costs of the action, together with a reasonable attorney's fee as determined by the court. On a finding by the court that an action under this section was brought in bad faith and for the purpose of harassment, the court may award to the defendant attorney's fees reasonable in relation to the work expended and costs.

(b) In determining the amount of liability in any action under subsection (a), the court shall consider, among other relevant factors --

> (1) in any individual action under subsection (a)(2)(A), the frequency and persistence of noncompliance by the debt collector, the nature of such noncompliance, and the extent to which such noncompliance was intentional; or

> (2) in any class action under subsection (a)(2)(B), the frequency and persistence of noncompliance by the debt collector, the nature of such noncompliance, the resources of the debt collector, the number

of persons adversely affected, and the extent to which the debt collector's noncompliance was intentional.

(c) A debt collector may not be held liable in any action brought under this title if the debt collector shows by a preponderance of evidence that the violation was not intentional and resulted from a bona fide error notwithstanding the maintenance of procedures reasonably adapted to avoid any such error.

(d) An action to enforce any liability created by this title may be brought in any appropriate United States district court without regard to the amount in controversy, or in any other court of competent jurisdiction, within one year from the date on which the violation occurs.

(e) No provision of this section imposing any liability shall apply to any act done or omitted in good faith in conformity with any advisory opinion of the Commission, notwithstanding that after such act or omission has occurred, such opinion is amended, rescinded, or determined by judicial or other authority to be invalid for any reason.

814. Administrative enforcement   [15 USC 1692l]

(a) Compliance with this title shall be enforced by the Commission, except to the extent that enforcement of the requirements imposed under this title is specifically committed to another agency under subsection (b). For purpose of the exercise by the Commission of its functions and powers under the Federal Trade Commission Act, a violation of this title shall be deemed an unfair or deceptive act or practice in violation of that Act. All of the functions and powers of the Commission under the Federal Trade Commission Act are available to the Commission to enforce compliance by any person with this title, irrespective of whether that person is engaged in commerce or meets any other jurisdictional tests in the Federal Trade Commission Act, including the power to enforce the provisions of this title in the same manner as if the violation had been a violation of a Federal Trade Commission trade regulation rule.

(b) Compliance with any requirements imposed under this title shall be enforced under --

(1) section 8 of the Federal Deposit Insurance Act, in the case of --

(A) national banks, by the Comptroller of the Currency;

(B) member banks of the Federal Reserve System (other than national banks), by the Federal Reserve Board; and

(C) banks the deposits or accounts of which are insured by the Federal Deposit Insurance Corporation (other than members of the Federal Reserve System), by the Board of Directors of the Federal Deposit Insurance Corporation;

(2) section 5(d) of the Home Owners Loan Act of 1933, section 407 of the National Housing Act, and sections 6(i) and 17 of the Federal Home Loan Bank Act, by the Federal Home Loan Bank Board (acting directing or through the Federal Savings and Loan Insurance Corporation), in the case of any institution subject to any of those provisions;

(3) the Federal Credit Union Act, by the Administrator of the National Credit Union Administration with respect to any federal credit union;

(4) subtitle IV of Title 49, by the Interstate Commerce Commission with respect to any common carrier subject to such subtitle;

(5) the Federal Aviation Act of 1958, by the Secretary of Transportation with respect to any air carrier or any foreign air carrier subject to that Act; and

(6) the Packers and Stockyards Act, 1921 (except as provided in section 406 of that Act), by the Secretary of Agriculture with respect to any activities subject to that Act.

(c) For the purpose of the exercise by any agency referred to in subsection (b) of its powers under any Act referred to in that subsection, a violation of any requirement imposed under this title shall be deemed to be a violation of a requirement imposed under that Act. In addition to its powers under any provision of law specifically referred to in subsection (b), each of the agencies referred to in that subsection may exercise, for the purpose of enforcing compliance with any requirement imposed under this title any other authority conferred on it by law, except as provided in subsection (d).

(d) Neither the Commission nor any other agency referred to in subsection (b) may promulgate trade regulation rules or other regulations with respect to the collection of debts by debt collectors as defined in this title.

815. Reports to Congress by the Commission [15 USC 1692m]

(a) Not later than one year after the effective date of this title and at one-year intervals thereafter, the Commission shall make reports to the Congress concerning the administration of its functions under this title, including such recommendations as the Commission deems necessary or appropriate. In addition, each report of the Commission shall include its assessment of the extent to which compliance with this title is being achieved and a summary of the enforcement actions taken by the Commission under section 814 of this title.

(b) In the exercise of its functions under this title, the Commission may obtain upon request the views of any other federal agency that exercises enforcement functions under section 814 of this title.

816. Relation to State laws [15 USC 1692n]

This title does not annul, alter, or affect, or exempt any person subject to the provisions of this title from complying with the laws of any state with respect to debt collection practices, except to the extent that those laws are inconsistent with any provision of this title, and then only to the extent of the inconsistency. For purposes of this section, a state law is not inconsistent with this title if the protection such law affords any consumer is greater than the protection provided by this title.

817. Exemption for State regulation   [15 USC 1692o]

The Commission shall by regulation exempt from the requirements of this title any class of debt collection practices within any state if the Commission determines that under the law of that state that class of debt collection practices is subject to requirements substantially similar to those imposed by this title, and that there is adequate provision for enforcement.

818. Effective date [15 USC 1692 note]

This title takes effect upon the expiration of six months after the date of its enactment, but section 809 shall apply only with respect to debts for which the initial attempt to collect occurs after such effective date (Approved September 20, 1977).

Chapter 16

Myth Busters

Myth 1: When collectors refuse my payments, the debt goes away and/or I am no longer obligated to pay!

Once an account goes delinquent, collectors and creditors can legally refuse your payments or payment offers. However, the debt does NOT go away!

This myth continues to grow because people are told, as soon as collectors and creditors refuse your "tender of payment" they forfeit the right to collect on the account and the debt is discharged.

This idea stems from the Uniform Commercial Code (UCC). This law is often misquoted leading people to believe that if a payment offer is refused, the debt is wiped out.

Using this logic, I could offer a $5 payment on a $10,000 debt and if the creditor or collector refused my offer, the debt would be discharged. If this were true, everyone would be making $5 offers and clearing their debts.

Here is the section of the Uniform Commercial Code (UCC) that is often misinterpreted:

U.C.C.—ARTICLE 3—NEGOTIABLE INSTRUMENTS, PART 6. DISCHARGE AND PAYMENT 3-603; TENDER OF PAYMENT:

(a) If tender of payment of an obligation to pay an instrument is made to a person entitled to enforce the instrument, the effect of tender is governed by principles of law applicable to tender of payment under a simple contract.

(b) If tender of payment of an obligation to pay an instrument is made to a person entitled to enforce the instrument and the tender is refused, there is discharge, to the extent of the amount of the tender, of the obligation of an indorser or accommodation party having a right of recourse with respect to the obligation to which the tender relates.

(c) If tender of payment of an amount due on an instrument is made to a person entitled to enforce the instrument, the obligation of the obligor to pay interest after the due date on   the amount tendered is discharged. If presentment is required with respect to an instrument and the obligor is able and ready to pay on the due date at every place of payment stated in the instrument, the obligor is deemed to have made tender of payment on the due date to the person entitled to enforce the instrument.

From my research, this law does NOT apply to the cancellation of credit contracts. Article 3-603(b) refers to the tender of payments using negotiable instruments (checks, bank drafts, and so forth) and, if the payment is refused, the amount of the tender is discharged.

**So, even if this rule did apply, the only amount that is discharged is the face value of the negotiable instrument. **

So what are your options when debt collectors refuse your payment offer?

First, there is no law that compels collectors to accept your payments or payment offers. There is also no law compelling you to accept collectors' demands.

Second, never negotiate with collectors on the phone. They are trained to **"control the ball"** (conversation) and so, unless you are a very skilled negotiator, you'll only end up frustrated, angry or scared.

Third, always check the Statute of Limitations (SoL) on the enforcement of a debt BEFORE making any payment offer.

Note: If you make a payment offer...PUT IT IN WRITING! It gives you and the collector a record of your "good faith" effort to resolve the issue.

If you have to defend your actions in court, putting things in writing becomes extremely important because judges want to see what you have done to take care of the debt. They love it when debtors can show a written payment offer that was refused by the collector.

In many cases, the judge will dismiss the case (not the debt) and tell the collector to work it out with you.

Send offers in writing because this places collectors in the position of accepting or declining your offer. Accepting your offer means you pay on your terms, declining your offer jeopardizes their ability to use the courts to enforce the debt.

If they accept your written offer, you'll probably never receive anything in writing that says they accept your plan however; the sample letter covers this with a statement that says:

"Please note that accepting (cashing) this payment constitutes a payment agreement between us according to the terms outlined above."

KEEP ACCURATE RECORDS! Keep copies of every letter you send and everything they send including envelopes.

What about creditors who refuse payments?

Most creditors will work with you if you call them BEFORE the account goes delinquent! Letting them know ahead of time shows that you care and helps to maintain your credibility. On the other hand, not all creditors will work with you in spite of a good previous payment history.

I've seen people miss a payment for the first time in 10 years and their creditor show no mercy.

Early intervention may get your creditor to:

Eliminate late charges on your account;

Not report your delinquency to credit reporting agencies

Permit you to make interest-only payments for awhile;

Prevent your utilities from being cut off

Not turn your account over to a collection agency;

Defer payments to the end of your contract;

Failing to contact your creditors is a big mistake because eventually they will call and demand the full balance or payments much higher than you can afford.

Keep in mind that, just like collectors, creditors are not compelled to accept your payment offer. The idea that they have to accept your payment or discharge the debt is a myth (see first paragraph of this myth). When creditors refuse payments, it's usually because company policy prohibits it or they fear future problems with legal actions. It can't hurt to ask and, if your first offer is declined, ask what they feel is an acceptable payment. You may have to negotiate hard but, what ever you do,

DO NOT agree to terms you cannot afford!

As a last resort, send a written payment offer anyway. I've seen creditors accept a written plan even after refusing your plan over the phone.

Myth 2: Debts cannot be sent to collections or reported to Credit Reporting Agencies without notifying me first.

The Truth…

Until recently, creditors were not required to notify debtors that they intend to report negative information or have reported negative information about the debtor's account to any credit bureau.

The New Fair and Accurate Credit Transactions Act of 2003 (FACTA) requires creditors to notify consumers when they intend to place negative information in their credit file or within 30 days of actually reporting the negative information.

Here's an excerpt from the FACTA…

SEC. 217. REQUIREMENT TO DISCLOSE COMMUNICATIONS TO A CONSUMER REPORTING AGENCY:

(a) IN GENERAL. Section 623(a) of the Fair Credit Reporting Act (15 U.S.C. 1681s2(a)) as amended by this Act, is amended by inserting after paragraph (6), the following new paragraph:

(7) NEGATIVE INFORMATION.

(A) NOTICE TO CONSUMER REQUIRED.

(i) IN GENERAL. If any financial institution that extends credit and regularly and in the ordinary course of business furnishes information to a consumer reporting agency described in section 603(p) furnishes negative information to such an agency regarding credit extended to a customer, the financial institution shall provide a notice of such furnishing of negative information, in writing, to the customer.

(ii) NOTICE EFFECTIVE FOR SUBSEQUENT SUBMISSIONS.

After providing such notice, the financial institution may submit additional negative information to a consumer reporting agency described in section 603(p) with respect to the same transaction, extension of credit, account, or customer without providing additional notice to the customer.

(B) TIME OF NOTICE.

IN GENERAL. The notice required under subparagraph (A) shall be provided to the customer prior to, or no later than 30 days after, furnishing the negative information to a consumer reporting agency described in section 603(p).

COORDINATION WITH NEW ACCOUNT DISCLOSURES.

If the notice is provided to the customer prior to furnishing the negative information to a consumer reporting agency, the notice may not be included in the initial disclosures provided under section 127(a) of the Truth in Lending Act.

(C) COORDINATION WITH OTHER DISCLOSURES.

The notice required under subparagraph (A) may be included on or with any notice of default, any billing statement, or any other materials provided to the customer; and must be clear and conspicuous.

The above information applies to Credit Reporting Agencies only!

It does not include collection agencies reporting delinquent account information. Presumably, this is because the debtor is fully aware of the delinquent account and the account was, more than likely, already reported as delinquent by the original creditor.

Also notice, the law does not address or require debtors to be notified before a delinquent account is sent to collections. So, a delinquent account can be sent to collections without any prior notification.

However, that does not mean that collectors can just report any thing they feel like reporting (although many do) to credit reporting agencies. The Truth in Lending Act (TILA) and the Uniformed Commercial Code (UCC) require all credit contracts to come with a disclosure statement that fully discloses and clearly spells out, in plain language, the terms of the credit contract.

This means your disclosure statement may contain a statement that requires you to be notified before or shortly after any negative information has been reported. The statement must clearly identify who must notify you (creditor or collector or both).

Additionally, some states have consumer laws that speak to full disclosure. Only if your credit disclosure statements call for it, are creditors obligated to notify you before sending a delinquent account to collections. Many disclosure statements do NOT require notification but may choose to do so but only as a courtesy.

The "Delinquent Information Being Reported Notice" can be included with your regular monthly statement (billing notice) so watch for this.

If your debt is past due and, included with your regular monthly statement is a statement or memo informing you of their intention to report your delinquent account to one or more credit reporting agencies, the creditor has meant the notification requirements of the FACTA.

The Bottom Line:

> Creditors do NOT have to tell you before sending an account to collections.

> Creditors can report your delinquent accounts to credit reporting agencies before telling you, however, they must inform you of their actions within 30 days after reporting the information.

> Collectors are NOT required to notify you before, during, or after reporting your delinquent accounts to credit reporting agencies.

> Visit my free site for more information:

> http://www.fair-credit-reporting.com/

Myth 3: Collectors must wait at least 30 days after initial notification before resuming collection activities.

This is absolutely **NOT** true! The 30-day rule applies to debtors NOT collectors!

Put another way, "Can debt collectors demand payment, or take legal action during the thirty (30) day period for disputing a debt?

YES! Section 809(b) permits collectors to demand payment or take legal action during the thirty-day period for disputing a debt when consumers have not notified the collection agency in writing that the debt is disputed.

The FDCPA treats the thirty-day time frame as a dispute period within which the consumer may insist that the collector verify the debt: not a grace period within which collection efforts are prohibited.

The collection agency must ensure, however, that its collection activity does not overshadow and is not inconsistent with the disclosure of the consumer's right to dispute the debt specified by Section 809(a).

Finally, once the debt is disputed in writing, ALL collection actions must cease until the collector verifies the debt.

The 30-day rule confuses a lot of people. I see it misinterpreted all the time, especially on-line by paralegals and even some attorneys.

The 30 days are for the debtor to dispute the debt. It does not prohibit collection efforts! Congress put in the 30-day time limit to give debtors time to gather information before responding to a collector's debt notification. It also lets the collector assume that, if the debtor has not responded within the 30 days, the debt must be valid.

This is why it's so important to dispute the debt the same day you receive a letter or call from a collector. The 30 day rule does not prohibit collectors from pursuing collection actions while waiting for you to respond.

Collectors only have to cease their collection efforts AFTER receiving a "dispute letter."

In summary, "The 30-day rule does NOT apply to collectors!"

Myth 4: Collectors can add whatever collection charges they want to a debt! (When no judgment exists)

Section 808 of the FDCPA makes it an unfair practice to collect:

"any amount (including any interest, fee, charge or expense...) unless such an amount is expressly authorized by the agreement creating the debt or permitted by State law."

Debt collectors may attempt to charge additional fees if either:

(A) The charge is expressly provided for in the contract creating the debt and the charge is not prohibited by state law, or

(B) The contract is silent but the charge is otherwise expressly permitted by state law. Conversely, debt collectors may not collect an additional amount if either:

(1) State law expressly prohibits collection of the amount or;

(2) The contract does not provide for collection of the amount and state law is silent.

(3) If state law permits collection of reasonable fees, the reasonableness (and consequential legality) of these fees is determined by state law.

(4) A debt collector may establish an "agreement" without a written contract. For example, he may collect a service charge on a dishonored check based on a posted sign on the merchant's premises allowing such a charge, if he can demonstrate that the consumer knew of the charge.

Interest on Debt (when a judgment exists)

States have their own rules for adding interest to judgments; sometimes called statutory charges, because the amount of interest is set by law. Typically, interest begins to accrue from the date the judgment is rendered until the judgment is paid in full.

Use this Garnishment Laws and Procedures link to learn about your State's interest rate on judgments. After locating your state's garnishment procedures, look at the "Interest Rate at which Judgments Accrue" section located just after the procedures. Use this link to read about

http://www.small-claims-courts.com/Wage-Garnishment-Laws.html

Interest on overdue taxes, child support and student loans

The interest on overdue federal taxes and defaulted student loans is set by federal law. Interest on overdue child support is set by state law.

See the IRS FAQ for information on overdue taxes.

www.irs.gov/faqs/index.html

Use this link to learn more about interest on defaulted student loans.

www.student-loan-default.com/faq.html

Use this calculator link to learn more about interest on child support.

www.child-support-collections.com/free-support-calculator.html

Legal Fees

Legal fees refer to charges for an attorney's services and may also include court costs such as filing fees.

Creditors typically add the legal costs of collecting a debt to the account balance.

There is a distinct difference between lawyers that are debt collectors and lawyers that are representing a creditor.

> **"An attorney or law firm whose efforts to collect consumer debts on behalf of its clients that regularly include activities traditionally associated with debt collection, such as sending demand letters (dunning notices) or making collection telephone calls to the consumer, are debt collectors and subject to the FDCPA"**

On the other hand, an attorney whose practice is limited to legal activities (e.g., the filing and prosecution of lawsuits to reduce debts to judgment) are generally exempt from the FDCPA but may still be liable under state collection laws.

In summary, if a judgment exists, then interest is added at the rate set by state law. In no judgment exists, collectors CANNOT just add whatever collection charges, fees or interest they want. They must follow the FDCPA, state law (if applicable), and the original contract.

Myth 5: "Collectors only have 30 days to validate debts!"

There are two very important points to make here:

Debt collectors ***DO NOT*** have to respond to your dispute!

If debt collectors do respond, they ***are NOT limited*** to only 30 days!

Let me address each point...

Point #1

The Fair Debt Collection Practices Act (FDCPA) does not require debt collectors to respond to a written dispute UNLESS the collector intends to continue his collection efforts.

This means that, if after receiving your written dispute, the collector decides NOT to pursue the debt; he is not obligated to send you anything. This explains why you never hear from most collectors after disputing an old debt.

Collectors buy old debts for pennies on the dollar. But, on debts more than a couple years old, the chances of the collector receiving any records from the original creditor are slim to none and collectors know this.

So, they contact you hoping to collect something. They are also hoping you do not know you have the right to dispute debts and the right to force collectors to either validate the debt or leave you alone.

When you dispute debts, collectors rarely waste time trying to locate records they know have been deleted, lost or destroyed, they simply bundle your debt along with hundreds more and sell them to the next collector for...you guessed it--pennies on the dollar.

This explains why you can dispute a debt with collector number one and then a couple months later receive a new collection notice from collector number two.

If this happens to you, your best course of action is to dispute the debt again in writing. Use the instructions and sample letters from my free site here: **www.debt-n-credit-letters.com/**

Point #2

The FDCPA does not limit collectors to 30 days for responding to your written dispute.

"Collectors have to respond to your written dispute ONLY IF they intend to pursue collection activities!"

If they decide to respond, they must follow the FDCPA validation rules by obtaining documents of proof from the original creditor and then send the documents to you. All of this must be done at the collector's expense.

In many cases, creditors fail to respond in a timely manner for a variety of reasons; lost records, deleted accounts, account too old, sold/transferred the debt and so forth.

I've seen it take as long as 14 months before a collector responds to a dispute letter. This is legal as long as the response complies with the FDCPA.

NOTE: During this period it is illegal for the collector to take any collection actions against you.

People often ask me what they can do when, after disputing a debt, the collector responds by sending a summons to appear in court.

My answer is always APPEAR IN COURT! Take proof that the collector received your dispute letter but failed to respond according to the FDCPA.

When the judge asks for your side of the story, tell the judge that you followed the FDCPA by disputing the debt in writing within the 30 days but the collector failed to respond with the information required in the FDCPA.

Provide the judge certified copies of your documents backing up your story. In most cases, the judge will stop the hearing and order the collector not to return to court until complying with the validation requirements of the FDCPA.

WARNING! **Do not fail to appear in court because doing so will more that likely result in a "default judgment" against you.**

Myth 6: Charged off debts are no longer collectible!

The IRS allows creditors to charge off debts under a rule called "Specific Charge-Off Method." In a nutshell, this rule allows creditors to take a loss on their income taxes when they feel the debt is currently uncollectible.

Although they charge off the debt, they can still attempt to collect the debt at a later date. If successful, they must claim the newly collected debt on the tax return of the year in which they successfully collect the debt.

Generally, before charging off a debt, creditors will try to collect the debt for up to 120 days (some may go as long as 9 months) through an in-house collection department. If unsuccessful, they send the account to a third party collector but retain legal rights to the account.

The 3rd party collector must act on behalf of the original creditor. If you dispute the debt with the 3rd party collector, the collector generally sends the account back to the creditor who may send it to another 3rd party collector or charge it off and then bundle your account with other delinquent accounts and sell the bundled debts on the Junk Debt Market.

When creditors sell your account, they also sell the rights to the account so only the new owner (debt collector) can collect the debt. However, this does not permit the new owner to report this as a new debt to the credit reporting agencies (but they do anyway). If they do, see my site to learn how to fix your credit reports at: **www.fair-credit-reporting.com/**

Once a company decides to charge off a debt, if they choose to report the debt to a credit reporting agency, they must do so within 90 days of the charged off date.

Delinquent debt accounts are bought and sold daily so your old account might end up in the hands of a dozen different debt collectors over the course of several years. This explains why you receive calls from debt collectors demanding payment on old forgotten debts.

Myth 7: Disposable income is what's left over after food, clothing, and shelter.

The term "Disposable Income" generally means after-tax income that is officially calculated as the difference between personal income and personal tax and non-tax payments. In other words, it's whatever money is left in your paycheck after all required taxes and national insurances have been deducted.

In general terms, personal tax and non-tax payments are about 15% of personal income, which makes disposable income about 85% of personal income.

When applying for certain state, federal, and private benefits and protections, the term "disposable income" may change slightly. For instance, when applying for loans, mortgages, credit cards and veterans home loans, disposable income is that income left over after paying all required taxes, national insurances and all essentials such as food, clothing, and shelter.

Some state and federal assistance programs look at disposable income as "any income available for spending and saving! Generally, this means money left over after taxes and fixed costs such as rent/mortgage, food, car payments, insurance, etc.

Disposable income is also defined as the total income that can be used by a household for either consumption or saving during a given period of time, usually one year.

Another way to define disposable income is that portion of an individual's income (wages and salaries, interest and dividend payments from financial assets, and rents and net profits from businesses as well as capital gains on real or financial assets) over which the recipient has complete discretion.

For the purposes of calculating whether you are entitled to federal, state and non-profit legal help and similar services; many states will deduct the following from your income:

a) Deduction of a certain amount depending on how many dependent children you have;

b) Tax and National Insurance;

c) Maintenance you are paying to your wife/husband or former wife/husband or a child or relative, (who are not members of your current household);

d) Housing costs for example mortgage or rent, (less any housing benefit). This also includes council tax, water rates, insurance premiums, and other costs associated with where you live. There is a maximum figure of $545 per month if you have no dependents. Otherwise the full value of your housing costs can be taken into account;

e) Employment related expenses, for example travel costs;

f) Childcare (babysitting) charges, these are only deductible if you are receiving a wage or salary and actually pay private childcare charges. Deduction can only be made for children 15 or under, (unless they are disabled in which case there will be no limit on age);

g) If you are in receipt of certain state benefits on top of your income then these will be disregarded, (examples are disability living allowance, invalid care allowance, council tax benefit, housing benefit, payments out of the social fund etc.).

Note: Disposable income was also known, in previous generations, as discretionary money.

Myth 8: There is a grace period before debts become delinquent.

All debts become delinquent or overdue the day after a payment is due and not paid.

Lenders offer "grace periods" that range from a few days to as many as 30 days, however these grace periods **DO NOT** mean the debt is not delinquent or overdue, it simply means the lender has agreed to wait a certain number of days before taking any action such as adding interest or calling you.

Check the fine print! The Truth in Lending Act requires full disclosure of all credit terms. If a creditor provides for a grace period it must be outlined in the credit contract and/or credit terms disclosure statement.

Read your credit terms disclosure statement carefully because most credit contracts, that include grace periods, continue to charge interest and, in many cases, at the highest interest rate allowed by law.

Nowadays, lenders (especially credit card companies) use your use of the grace period as an excuse to raise your interest rate. Keep in mind that many lenders charge an additional fee (usually called a late fee) and so any payment made after the due date is first applied toward the late fee, then toward the outstanding or unpaid interest, then toward the current interest and finally (if there is anything left) toward the outstanding balance.

> **Note: In most cases, the delinquent date and the date the statute of limitations to collect the debt begins running are the same day. This is also the date that should be reported to credit reporting agencies and credit bureaus.**

Many junk debt buyers buy old debts and then report the debt as a new debt. This is illegal and, although collectors are supposed to correct the inaccurate information, they rarely comply with the law. Thus, it's left up to you to dispute your credit reports to have the inaccurate information corrected or removed. Learn how to correct your reports here: **www.fair-credit-reporting.com/**

Myth 9: Student Loans cannot be collected after 6 years of delinquency.

This is no longer true!

The Statute of Limitations on collecting defaulted student loans was eliminated by the Higher Education Act. Section 484A removes all limitations and gives the Department of Education or the guaranty agency (bank or lender) the ability to file suit, enforce judgments, initiate offsets, or other actions, to collect a defaulted student loan regardless of the age of the debt.

Therefore, Statute of Limitations is no longer a valid defense against repayment of student loans. Here are some additional tips:

1. No Fees: You cannot be charged application fees or prepayment penalties when consolidating student loans!

2. No Credit Checks: Consolidating student loans is a FREE government program that does not require credit checks. (Exception: PLUS borrowers are subject to a check for adverse credit history.)

3. Payback Period: The payback term ranges from 10 to 30 years, depending on the amount of education debt being repaid and the repayment option you select. Other education loans not included in the consolidation loan are considered in determining the maximum payback period.

4. Interest Rates: Federal statute sets the interest rate on consolidated student loans at NO HIGHER THAN 1/8th of a percent more than the effective rate on your individual loans fixed for the life of the loan thus; you are protected from future increases in variable rate loans!

5. Repayment Options: There are three basic repayment options for consolidation loans:

(1) Level-repayment; equal-installments;

(2) Graduated repayment: increases over time; and

(3) Income-based payment plans: increases/decreases based on income.

6. Repayment Incentives: Repayment incentives come in the form of lower interest rates and/or rebates and are based on your on-time repayment history and payment amount. Higher payments mean sooner payoff which equals better incentives.

7. Tax Credits: Two federal income taxes credits dollar-for-dollar reductions in tax liability and are available for higher education expenses.

(1) The Hope tax credit, worth up to $1,500 per student, is available to first and second year students enrolled at least half time.

(2) The Lifetime Learning tax credit is equal to 20 percent of a family's tuition expenses, up to $5,000, for virtually any post-secondary education and training, including subsequent undergraduate years, graduate and professional schools, and even less than half time study. Also, interest on student loans might be tax deductible!

Learn more about defaulted student loans on my FREE Site…

http://www.student-loan-default.com/

Myth 10: Once the Debt Collection Statute of Limitations (SoL) expires on a debt, it must be removed from my credit reports.

This is just not true! The SoL for enforcing the collection of debts is different from the time limits for reporting negative information on credit reports.

Generally, credit report information is reported for 7 or 10 years depending on the type of debt. On the other hand, the SoL for enforcing the collection of some debts may be as short as 2 years or as long as 21 years when judgments are involved.

See this page for in-depth information on credit reporting periods:

http://www.fair-credit-reporting.com/credit-laws/credit-reporting-periods.html

See this page for in-depth information on enforcing debt collection periods (SoL):

http://www.fair-debt-collection.com/statue-limitations-explained.html

Myth 11: Using the IRS Form 1099 is legal

Collectors who send letters with the heading "IRS Statutory Notification Letter—Publication 908" and reference the IRS Form 1099 are clearly violating section 807(5) "False threats of legal action" of the Fair Debt Collection Practices Act.

Typically, you'll receive an official looking letter that reminds you of a debt that you have failed to pay. It then refers to the creditor's "right to forgive this debt and submit a Form 1099 to the Internal Revenue Service on all bad debt accounts."

The last sentence usually reassures you that the creditor does not intend to take such an action at the time, and then urges you to remit payment to "avoid any additional collection activity."

First, the IRS does not require a creditor who discharges a debt to file a Form 1099, no matter how much the debt is worth. Second, although implied, the creditor rarely files a Form 1099 even when the debt remains unpaid.

In general, Form 1099 is used to report additional income. Let's say you owe a creditor $10,000 and the creditor files a Form 1099. This would mean that you, in theory, must report the $10,000 as income on your federal tax return. If the creditor does file this form (and only the creditor can file it) the creditor, NOT the Collector, must notify you.

Thus, the official looking letter you receive from collectors creates the distinct but false impression that the collection agency is required by the IRS or by a statute administered by the IRS to send that dunning letter to you.

Since this is not true, the representation violates Section 807(10). This, in turn, may create the additional false impression that the IRS has been informed about the debt at issue, also in violation of Section 807(10).

The whole intent behind the letter is to scare you into paying the debt but since the filing of such a form is never the result of a failure to pay and since the creditor does not ever intend to file such a form, a representation to the contrary, such as in the letter you receive, violates section 807(5).

Additionally, section 807(9) prohibits documents that fraudulently appear to be officially authorized by the government or otherwise mislead the recipient as to their authorship.

The purpose of this section is to discourage debt collectors from attempting to use the authority of the government deceptively to scare consumers into paying the debt at issue.

Thus, dunning consumers with letters that look like government documents violates both the letter and the spirit of this provision.

Myth 12: Divorce decrees can make ex-spouses responsible for debts outlined in the divorce agreement.

Divorce decrees only spell out who is supposed to pay the debt! They CANNOT and DO NOT legally change who is responsible for the debt. If your name is still on the credit contract then, in spite of what the divorce decree states, you are still responsible for the debt.

Whether you are responsible for your ex-spouse's debts depends on the circumstances surrounding the issue.

When couples divorce, they usually agree on who pays certain debts. For example, a car loan is in both names and the divorce agreement states that the ex-wife keeps the car and is responsible for making the payments. Thus, they don't bother to redo the credit contract to remove the ex-husband's name.

Several months later, when the ex-wife defaults on the car loan, collectors start calling her and her ex-husband. The ex-husband claims that the debt is not his because his ex-wife got the car and the responsibility for payment in the divorce.

The collector says it is the ex-husband's responsibility and claims he will pursue legal action if the ex-husband does not pay. In this case the collector (or creditor) is correct and will win in court because the ex-husband is still on the credit contract and can be held accountable in spite of what the divorce decree states.

Divorced couples would be wise to have joint credit contracts revised so that only the name of the person responsible for the debt is on the contract. Just be prepared for the creditor to deny your request to remove one of the names.

Creditors are reluctant to remove any names, especially after a divorce, because experience tells them the chances are high that the loan will become delinquent. Having two people's names on the contract is better for the creditor because if one ex-spouse defaults, the lender can still pursue the other ex-spouse.

Along the same lines, ex-spouses usually demand to know why they were not notified before a debt became delinquent or shortly afterwards.

Creditors only have to senda delinquent notice to the address they have on file which is usually the address before the divorce.

It's a good bet you are not getting payment notices because you did not change the mailing address with the creditor. Whatever the case, creditors are not responsible for tracking people down in order to send payment notices. They are only required to send notices to the last known address.

It is the debtor's responsibility to keep the creditor informed of his or her whereabouts and for keeping the debt current.

Your best protection is to make sure your creditors know the current address of both ex-spouses listed on joint credit accounts. Also, make sure the lender knows you want to be notified as soon as possible before (or as soon as) an account becomes delinquent.

Doing this may prevent the account from being sent to collections and from being reported as a negative on your credit reports.

What happens when an ex-spouse goes bankrupt?

Just as in the previous paragraph, if there were no joint debts, you have nothing to worry about and your credit will not be affected. However, if there were any joint debts with your name still on the contract, then you can be held responsible for the entire debt. The bankruptcy discharge releases only the person granted the discharge from responsibility for repaying the debt.

Myth 13: Social Security Income (SSI) cannot be garnished.

According to the Social Security Administration website, Social Security benefits are generally exempt from execution, levy, attachment, garnishment, or other legal process, or from the operation of any bankruptcy or insolvency law.

What can be garnished?

(1) The Secretary of the Treasury can make levies for the collection of delinquent Federal taxes and under certain circumstances delinquent child support payments; and

(2) An individual may use garnishment or a similar legal process to enforce a child support or alimony obligation.

Section 207 of the Social Security Act provides:

"The right of any person to any future payment under this title shall not be transferable or assignable, at law or in equity, and none of the moneys paid or payable or rights existing under this title shall be subject to execution, levy, attachment, garnishment, or other legal process, or to the operation of any bankruptcy or insolvency law."

However, section 6331 of the Internal Revenue Code of 1954 (26 U.S.C. 6331) which was enacted into law on August 16, 1954, after the enactment of section 207, gives the Secretary of the Treasury the right to levy or seize for collection of delinquent Federal taxes, property, rights to property, whether real or personal, tangible, or intangible and the right to make successive levies and seizures until the amount due, together with all expenses, is fully paid.

References: SSR 79-4: SECTIONS 207, 452(b), 459 and 462(f) (42 U.S.C. 407, 652(b), 659 and 662(f)) LEVY AND GARNISHMENT OF BENEFITS 20 CFR 404.970 SSR 79-4, See the full code here:

www.ssa.gov/OP_Home/rulings/oasi/41/SSR79-04-oasi-41.html

Special Rule Change:

The Social Security Administration (SSA) recently changed its rules to allow the collection of overdue Program and Administrative Debts using Administrative Wage Garnishment!

The regulations dealing with the collection of program overpayment debts that arise under titles II and XVI of the Social Security Act (the Act) and administrative debts owed to the SSA have been modified.

Specifically, the change establishes new regulations on the use of administrative wage garnishment (AWG) to collect such debts when they are past due.

AWG is a process whereby the SSA orders the debtor's employer to withhold and pay the SSA up to 15 percent of the debtor's disposable pay every payday until the debt is repaid. The employer is required by law to comply with the AWG order.

These new rules are effective January 22, 2004. (References: SOCIAL SECURITY ADMINISTRATION 20 CFR Parts 404, 416 and 422 RIN 0960-AE92 Federal Old-Age, Survivors, and Disability Insurance and Supplemental Security Income).

Read the full text of the Debt Collection Improvement Act:

www.fms.treas.gov/debt/dmdcia.txt

Myth 14: Judgment proof means collectors must cease collection activity.

First, let's define Judgment Proof:

Judgment-proof is the commonly used term but a more accurate term would be "execution-proof"! Although creditors and debt collectors win lawsuits, they still have to collect. Therefore, if you are penniless you are insulated not from judgment but from execution (collection of the debt).

If you lose your "judgment proof" status due to new employment, the creditor or collector can:

1. Seek a judgment if they have not already done so; and

2. With judgment in hand, seek wage garnishment of up to 25% of your disposable income. (10% in cases of defaulted student loans)

Once you're employed again, it's better to negotiate a reduced payoff rather than risk a court-ordered judgment. The difference is your credit report will show "debt settled" instead of the more negative "judgment!

When am I Judgment Proof?

You may be considered "Judgment Proof" during periods of unemployment or while drawing disability pay or disability retired pay. Also, if you have no assets such as home, car, land, and other big-ticket items. In other words, you have no money and can prove it!

> **WARNING!   Never ignore a lawsuit or court appearance notice just because you are broke or have no assets! You must always respond to a lawsuit! If a debt collector or creditor is trying to sue and you believe that you are judgment proof, respond to the lawsuit as such.**

Failure to appear and show the judge why you are judgment proof opens the door for the judge to grant the creditor or collector a Default Judgment.

Even though they cannot collect anything from you now, collectors can wait many years and try again. Also, judgments show up on your credit report and are considered very negative.

A final note about judgment proof: whenever you anticipate becoming judgment proof (loss of income, divorce, and disability) it's best to let the creditor and/or collectors know about your situation right away. Use the free sample letters on my site to notify creditors and collectors:

www.debt-n-credit-letters.com/

Disability Payments:

In most states, State paid disability and private disability insurance payments are exempt from garnishment. The exceptions are generally for current and back child support payments and taxes. Most retired disability is exempt. To be sure, always call your State Attorney General's consumer protection division to find out the rules surrounding your situation.

Myth 15: Medical Bills are exempt from the FDCPA and Insurance Companies are responsible for paying them!

Medical Bills

Medical debts fall under the Fair Debt Collection Practices Act because medical debt meets the definition of a "debt" under rule 803(5).

This rule defines "debt" as:

"a consumer's obligation to pay money arising out of a transaction in which the money, property, insurance, or services are primarily for personal, family, or household purposes."

The rule goes on to state the term "debt" includes overdue medical bills that were originally payable in full within a certain time period (e.g., 30 days).

So, never let debt collectors tell you the medical debt they are collecting is exempt from the FDCPA.

Medical Insurance

Two common misunderstandings are:

1) The insurance company is responsible for paying my medical bills; and

2) Medical providers are required to bill your insurance company.

The truth is consumers are ultimately responsible for ensuring their debts are paid and remain current. Although most medical providers offer to submit the bill to your insurance company, you are still responsible for ensuring the insurance forms are correct and submitted in a timely manner.

It also means you must follow up in a timely manner to ensure the insurance company received the bill and actually paid the medical provider.

Most medical providers bill your insurance company for you as a convenience but accepting their offer does not relieve you of the responsibility of ensuring the medical bill gets paid.

It's not uncommon for medical providers to submit medical bills after the insurance company's deadline for submitting claims. In many cases and for a number of odd reasons, medical providers forget to submit the medical bill.

Regardless of the reason why the medical provider failed to submit the bill, you are ultimately responsible for paying the medical debt.

In some cases, your insurance company may reject the bill or flat out refuse to pay. If this happens, the medical provider will expect you to pay the bill and, unless you've disputed the debt with the medical provider, you are expected to pay the bill in a timely manner.

The fact that your insurance company did not pay is not your medical provider's concern; it's up to you to pay the medical provider and then submit claims, to collect whatever amount you are entitled too, from your insurance company .

Always read the medical provider's paperwork carefully before signing anything.

Medical Bill Disputes

Medical bills and old medical debts can be disputed just like any other debt. Use the information in this guide and from my free websites to dispute medical debts and to negotiate down the final payoff.

Medical Debts and Interest

Just like any debt, interest can be added to medical bills IF the original contract or paperwork allows it AND your state law does not prohibit it.

Even if the original paperwork does allow it, ALWAYS check your state laws to ensure you are not being overcharged. Some states limit the amount of interest and the amount of collection fees.

Statute of Limitations on Medical Debts

Medical debts are generally considered closed-ended credit contracts with a definite pay-off time limit. Unless you have a separate agreement, medical debts are usually payable at the time services are rendered or, in some cases within 30 days.

Thus, failure to pay a medical debt is treated just like any other debt and the legal enforcement of the debt can expire. Always check your State's Statute of Limitations (SoL) before paying old medical debts.

Myth 16: Liens placed on my home will force me to sell it.

Real property (land and buildings on the land) cannot be seized and sold to satisfy a lien. On the other hand, in some states personal property that you own outright (does not secure a loan) such as unsecured cars, televisions, stereos and so forth can be seized and then sold to satisfy a lien.

Definition of Creditor's or Collector's Lien

A legal right or interest that a creditor or other person(s) have in another's property and lasting until the debt that the lien secures is paid.

Definition of Mechanic's Lien

The right of a craftsman, laborer, supplier, architect or other person who has worked upon improvements or delivered materials to a particular parcel of real estate (either as an employee of the owner or as a sub-contractor to a general contractor) to place a lien on that real property for the value of the services and/or materials if not paid.

Numerous other technical laws surround mechanic's liens, including requirements of prompt written notice to the owner of the property (even before the general contractor has been tardy in making payment), limits on the amount collectible in some states, and various time limitations to enforce the lien.

Ultimate, last-resort enforcement of the mechanic's lien is accomplished by filing a lawsuit to foreclose the lien and have the property sold in order to be paid.

Property owners should make sure that their general contractors pay their employees or subcontractors to avoid a mechanic's lien, since the owner could be forced to pay the debts of a general contractor even though the owner has already paid the contractor. If the worker or supplier does not sue to enforce the mechanic's lien, he/she may still sue for the debt.

The term mechanic's lien is also referred to as "material man's lien" and "construction lien" and used when improvements, repairs, or maintenance is performed on real property.

Creditors, debt collectors, and ordinary citizens can petition courts to grant a judgment and then place a lien on a debtor's "Real Property."

If granted it's called a "Judgment Lien", and places an encumbrance on the property so that, if the property is sold and the primary (and secondary) lien holder(s) (mortgage or loan company) is paid in full, left over funds are used to pay any taxes first and the rest, if any is used to pay down or pay off the lien.

> **Note: The term "Real Property" is legally distinguished from "Personal Property." Land is called real property. Personal property is also called chattels (defined as any property—consumable or non-consumable, tangible or intangible) and is property other than the land itself.**

If you receive a "notice of a lien," ALWAYS respond! If the lien surprises you, immediately check with the court that issued the lien and see if a mistake was made. Request copies of all court documents and look for any discrepancies and, if any exist, consider filing a petition to rehear the case. You might just get the case overturned.

Remember ***DO NOT fail*** to respond!

Liens on Real Property: Liens on a house, real property liens, judgment liens and state or federal tax liens all mean the same basic thing as described above. However, it's important to note that tax liens take priority over all other liens placed on a property. So, if your property already has a lien from a credit card company and then later on a tax lien is placed against the property, the tax lien gets paid first after any mortgages are satisfied.

Myth 17: It's illegal for collectors to leave collection messages on home answering machines.

Home Answering Machines

Collectors can leave messages on personal answering machines located in your home, even though other family members or visiting friends and relatives might hear the message.

A legal message might go like this:

> "This is Mr. Collector with Default Collections. I'm calling about your overdue credit card payment. It's urgent that you return my call today so we can discuss bringing your account current. My phone number is 555-1234."

In reality a message does not need to contain any information other than the name of the caller and a number to call back but leaving comments such as "it's urgent" or "it's important" and leaving a brief reason for the call does not violate the law.

Collectors who call several times a day and leave a brief message because they did not actually speak with the debtor do not violate the FDCPA.

Collectors who call and, after speaking with you or your spouse, call again that day without a reasonable purpose for the call, are guilty of harassment.

Leaving threatening or abusive messages including abusive language, religious slurs, profanity, obscenity, calling the consumer a liar or a deadbeat, or other name calling, threatening legal action that they do not intend to take and the use of racial or sexual epithets are serious violations of the FDCPA.

> **Special Note: Making threats to children is an especially grievous violation of the FDCPA and should not go unreported. Immediately report collectors who threaten you, your children, or anyone associated with you, to your State Attorney General.**

Answering Machines at Work

Unless told otherwise, collectors can call you at work. Once informed that your employer objects to the calls, collectors must never call your workplace again.

The following information assumes the collector has NOT been told to stop calling yet.

If your work phone has a private voice mail feature or it has an answering machine attachment that no one else can access, then collectors can leave messages on it. The same rules about the type of message and content as outlined above still apply...threatening or abusive messages are illegal.

On the other hand, if you use a phone at work that can be accessed by anyone else, it's considered a public use phone and collectors must be very careful about the type of message they leave on public use phones.

They can leave messages but NO reference to the debt or the debt collector's business or any words that would indicate the call is about a debt. About the only things public messages can include are the collector's name, number and request to call back.

The tone of the message must be non-threatening. Even a tiny hint that the call is about the collection of a debt is illegal!

Calling repeatedly (one right after the other or within a short period of time) and leaving messages also violates the FDCPA.

Myth 18: The Soldiers and Sailors Act protects all military members from collection actions.

The Soldiers and Sailors Civil Relief Act of 1940 (SSCRA) is a law that protects active duty service members and it was recently updated and amended. It's now called the Service members Civil Relief Act of 2003 (SCRA).

There is a great deal of misunderstanding about this law. Many people mistakenly believe that it protects them anytime they are on active duty and anytime they are stationed outside the United States on official military orders.

This is not the case

Protections depend on the situation and must be considered on a case by case basis. For instance, if you have a situation in which you are being sued or someone is attempting to collect a debt from you, the SCRA may offer full, partial or no protection.

Any member of the uniformed services serving on active duty is covered under the Act including Reserve and Coast Guard members called to active duty, as well as officers of the Public Health Service and the National Oceanic and Atmospheric Administration.

If you are on active duty, you are under the protection of the Soldiers and Sailors Relief Act from the day you enter active duty until the day you separate.

If you have a credit card, mortgage, loans, car payments, pay rent for dependents or face potential civil litigation, you have the potential to benefit from the act.

The Service members Civil Relief Act of 2003, covers such issues as rental agreements, security deposits, prepaid rent, eviction, installment contracts, credit card interest rates, mortgage interest rates, mortgage foreclosure, civil judicial proceedings, and income tax payments.

It also provides many important protections to military members while on active duty. The SCRA protects active duty military members and reservists or members of the National Guard called to active duty (starting on the date active duty orders are received) and, in limited situations, dependents of military members (e.g., certain eviction actions).

To receive protection under some parts of the SCRA, the member must be prepared to show that military service has had a "material effect" on the legal or financial matter involved.

Protection under the SCRA must be requested during the member's military duty or within 30 to 180 days after military service ends, depending on the protection being requested.

In many situations, the SCRA protections are not automatic, but require some action to invoke the Act. For example, to obtain a reduction of your pre-active duty mortgage or credit card interest rates, you should send your lender/creditor a written request and a copy of your mobilization orders.

If you think that you have rights under the SCRA that may have been violated, or that you are entitled to be shielded from a legal proceeding or financial obligation by the SCRA protections, you should discuss the matter with a legal assistance attorney or a civilian lawyer as soon as possible.

How does the 6 % interest rule work?

For example, one of the most widely known benefits under the SSCRA and now the SCRA is the ability to reduce pre-service consumer debt and mortgage interest rates to 6% under certain circumstances.

Consider this example: Three months ago Mr. Smith and his wife bought a car for $13,000, paying $1,000 down and financing $12,000 at 9% interest. Last week, Mr. Smith was called to active duty as Staff Sergeant (SSG) Smith.

Before entering active duty Mr. Smith earned $42,000 per year. As a staff sergeant with over 12 years of military service he now earns only about $27,000.

Because of the SCRA, SSG Smith may ask the car financing company to lower the interest rate to 6% while he is on active duty because his military service has materially affected his ability to pay since he is earning less money on active duty than before.

SSG Smith should inform the finance company of his situation in writing with a copy of the orders to active duty attached, and request immediate confirmation that they have lowered his interest rate to 6% under the SCRA. The finance company must adjust the interest down to 6% unless it goes to court.

In court, the finance company, not SSG Smith, would have to prove that SSG Smith's ability to pay the loan has not been materially affected by his military service.

The 3% difference is forgiven or excused, and SSG Smith need not pay that amount.   SSG Smith does need to continue making the monthly payments of principal and interest (at 6%) to avoid his account being considered delinquent.   Continuing payments should also avoid any adverse credit reports from the finance company. (See Section 207, SCRA)

> **Important Note: In some situations civilian employers have agreed to pay the military member the difference between the military pay and the civilian pay earned before the call to active duty. In most such situations, military service has not materially affected the member's ability to pay so it is unlikely that the SCRA 6% interest limitation applies.**

Of course, if the military member's expenses increased (for example, the member must pay for a second apartment at the duty station, or the member's spouse gave up her job to move with him) military service might have materially affected the member and the SCRA 6% interest limit could apply.

But what if instead of buying the car before he came on active duty, SSG Smith left his car at home for his wife and purchased a used car at his duty station. To do so, he borrowed $4,000 at 9% interest. Since SSG Smith took this debt after entering active duty the SCRA 6% interest limit does not apply.

If you think being called to active military service has reduced your ability to meet your financial obligations, contact the nearest military legal assistance office to see if the SCRA applies.

Delay of Court and Administrative Proceedings

A major change provided by the SCRA is that it permits active duty service members, who are unable to appear in a court or administrative proceeding due to their military duties, to postpone the proceeding for a mandatory minimum of ninety days upon the service member's request.

The request must:

1. Be in writing;

2. Explain why the current military duty materially affects the service members ability to appear;

3. Provide a date when the service member can appear; and

4. Include a letter from the commander stating that the service member's duties preclude his or her appearance and that he is not authorized leave at the time of the hearing. This letter or request to the court will not constitute a legal appearance in court. Further delays may be granted at the discretion of the court, and if the court denies additional delays, an attorney must be appointed to represent the service member. (See Section 202, SCRA)

Termination of Leases:

Another significant change provided in the SCRA, is found in Section 305. The prior law only allowed the termination of pre-service "dwelling, professional, business, agricultural, or similar" leases.

The new provision in the SCRA allows termination of leases by active duty service members who subsequently receive orders for a permanent change of station (PCS) or a deployment for a period of 90 days or more.

The SCRA also includes automobiles leased for personal or business use by service members and their dependents. The pre-service automobile lease may be cancelled if the service member receives active duty orders for a period of one hundred and eighty (180) days or more. The automobile lease entered into while the service member is on active duty may be terminated if the service member receives Permanent Change of Station orders to:

1. Location outside the continental United States; or

2. Deployment orders for a period of one hundred and eighty days or more. (See Section 305, SCRA)

Eviction for Nonpayment of Rent

Although the SCRA does not excuse soldiers from paying rent, it does afford some relief if military service makes payment difficult. Military members and their dependents (in their own right) have some protection from eviction under the Service members Civil Relief Act (SCRA), Section 301.

The landlord must obtain a court order to evict a military member or his/her dependents. The court must find the member's failure to pay is not materially affected by his/her military service.

Material effect is present where the service member does not earn sufficient income to pay the rent. Where the member is materially affected by military service, the court may stay the eviction (three months unless the court decides on a shorter or longer period in the interest of justice) when the military member or dependents request it.

There is no requirement that the lease be entered into before entry on active duty, and the court could make any other just order under 301 of the SCRA.

The requirements of this section are:

1. The landlord is attempting eviction during a period in which the service member is in military service or after receipt of orders to report to duty;

2. The rented premises is used for housing by the spouse, children, or other dependents of the service member; and

3. The agreed rent does not exceed $2,400 per month.

Military members threatened with eviction for failure to pay rent should see a legal assistance attorney. (The amount is subject to change in future years and as of 2004 the ceiling is $2465.00)

Default Judgment Protection

If a default judgment is entered against a service member during his or her active duty service, or within 60 days thereafter, the SCRA allows the service member to reopen that default judgment and set it aside.

In order to set aside a default judgment, the service member must show that he or she was prejudiced by not being able to appear in person, and that he or she has good and legal defenses to the claims against him/her.

The service member must apply to the court for relief within 90 days of the termination or release from military service. (See Section 201, SCRA)

Life Insurance Protection

The SCRA also permits the service member to request deferment of certain commercial life insurance premiums and other payments for the period of military service and two years thereafter. If the Department of Veteran Affairs approves the request, the United States will guarantee the payments, the policy shall continue in effect, and the service member will have two years after the period of military service to repay all premiums and interest.

The SCRA increases the amount of insurance this program will cover to the greater of $250,000.00 or the maximum limit of the Service members Group Life Insurance. (See Section 401, SCRA)

State Taxation Clarification

The SCRA provides that a nonresident service member's military income and personal property are not subject to state taxation if the service member is present in the state only due to military orders.

The state is also prohibited from using the military pay of these nonresident service members to increase the state income tax of the spouse.

Under prior law, some states did not tax the nonresident service member directly, but did include the nonresident service member's income in the spouse's income, resulting in higher taxes for the spouse. (See Section 511, SCRA)

Health Insurance Reinstatement

The SCRA further provides for the reinstatement of any health insurance upon termination or release from service. The insurance must have been in effect before such service commenced and terminated during the period of military service.

The reinstatement of the health insurance is not subject to exclusions or a waiting period if the medical condition in question arose before or during the period of service, the exclusion or waiting period did not apply during coverage, and the medical condition has not been determined by the Secretary of the Veteran Affairs to be a disability incurred or aggravated by military service.

The reinstatement of health insurance protection does not apply to a service member entitled to participate in employer-offered insurance (See rules regarding employer offered health insurance care in the Uniformed Services Employment and Re-employment Act).

And finally, the service member must apply for the reinstatement of the health insurance within 120 days after termination or release from military service. As always submit such request to the insurance company in writing with a copy of the orders for active duty and release from active duty. (See Section 704, SCRA)

Statutes of Limitation (sec. 206)

(a). Tolling Of Statutes Of Limitation During Military Service:

The period of a service member's military service may not be included in computing any period limited by law, regulation, or order for the bringing of any action or proceeding in a court, or in any board, bureau, commission, department, or other agency of a State (or political subdivision of a State) or the United States by or against the service member or the service member's heirs, executors, administrators, or assigns.

(b). Redemption of Real Property:

A period of military service may not be included in computing any period provided by law for the redemption of real property sold or forfeited to enforce an obligation, tax, or assessment.

(c). Inapplicability to Internal Revenue Laws:

This section does not apply to any period of limitation prescribed by or under the internal revenue laws of the United States. Service members involved in civil litigation can request a delay in proceedings if they can show their military responsibilities preclude their proper representation in court.

This provision is most often invoked by service members who are on an extended deployment or stationed overseas. If you receive notice of court proceedings DO NOT do anything until you've contacted your unit or installation legal office.

Myth 19: Re-aging credit card debt is a scam!

Re-aging credit card and other types of credit accounts is an accepted and legal industry practice. It means your creditor re-sets the delinquent account back to current.

Let's say you are 5 months behind on your credit card bill and your creditor agrees to re-age your account.

This sounds great and it is possible to have your accounts re-aged but not all creditors are willing to do so. Also, creditors must follow federal guidelines when deciding whether or not to re-age delinquent accounts.

> **WARNING! Creditors may only re-age your account once in a 12-month period and twice in a five-year period for open-ended accounts (credit cards, charge cards, store cards etc.).**

To be considered for re-aging:

1. You must demonstrate a renewed willingness and ability to pay;

2. Your credit card account should be at least 9 months old;

3. You need to make at least three consecutive minimum monthly payments.

Creditors DO NOT have to re-age past due accounts. Some creditors never re-age accounts, some will only re-age an account one time, and other creditors follow the federal guidelines that allow once in a 12-month period or twice every five years. It all depends on the creditor's re-aging policy.

Some creditors will re-age past due accounts if you agree to enter a debt-workout program or debt-management plan. Once enrolled in a debt-management program, creditors typically charge lower interest rates; stop charging late fees and re-age the account (bring it current).

Be careful! Only sign up with a debt management company that you can trust. There are thousands of credit-counseling and debt-consolidation companies looking to make a quick buck by preying on stressed-out, financially vulnerable consumers.

Some companies are guilty of shoddy service and sky-high fees and others are just plain scams.

Don't ask for re-aging if you will not be able to keep up with the payments. In other words, don't waste your re-aging opportunity! It's better to wait until you can truly keep up the payments before approaching your creditors and asking them to re-age your account.

When asking creditors to re-age your accounts, be sure to get it in writing! If your creditor won't put the details of your re-aging program in writing, do it yourself. Keep a record of the conversation and send a copy of it to your creditor (keep a copy for yourself). Just remember, unless the creditor signs the agreement, you really don't have an agreement.

Myth 20: Collectors cannot collect after the Statute of Limitations on the collection of a debt expires.

This is absolutely false! Collectors can always **_try_** to collect debts even though the Statute of Limitations for enforcing them has expired.

In fact, if collectors take you to court and you fail to invoke the Statute of Limitations defense, the court is likely to grant collectors a judgment.

Even if collectors do not go to court, an expired Statute of Limitations does not prohibit collectors from trying to collect the debt by other means such as calling and sending dunning letters.

Collectors Often Try for Judgments on Old Debts!

The statute of limitations for the collection of debts is not well known and is often misunderstood. Actually the term, statute of limitations for the collection of debts is misleading.

The proper wording is, "statute of limitations for enforcing the collection of debts!" Let me be perfectly clear here! Even though the statute of limitations has expired, you can still be hauled into court!

That's why you must appear in court and raise the expired statute of limitations (SoL) defense. You can win but YOU must be present in court AND you must be the one to bring it up!

If you fail to show up, collectors will win by default! This default judgment then gives the collector a long time to pursue you and collect a debt that, had you showed up and mentioned the expired statute of limitations, would not be collectible.

WARNING! **Quite often collectors will convince you to make a "token payment," and then, they quietly seek a judgment against you. Underhanded collectors have been known to provide the court with your old address so you never receive the "notice to appear in court." When you fail to show up, the judge grants a "default judgment." The first time you are even aware of a judgment is when your bank account is seized or your wages are garnished!**

IMPORTANT INSTRUCTIONS: If you discover you're a victim of a default judgment, immediately get copies of the court papers filed by the collector and look for any misinformation, especially an outdated address.

If you can show that the collector used the wrong information to file the court petition, you can file for a rehearing and prove to the judge that the collector knew of your whereabouts but failed to provide the court that information.

By doing this, you stand a good chance of having the default judgment overturned. After all, you must be given due process and if the court appearance notice was sent to the wrong address, you must be given an opportunity to defend yourself in court. It is possible to have a default judgment reversed!

The bottom line is that it is NOT illegal for collectors to attempt to collect debts (unless they were discharged in bankruptcy) even though the statute of limitations has expired.

You must understand that collectors can still take you to court to try and enforce the collection of debts but, if you raise the "Expired Statute of Limitations" defense, and you have meant your state's qualifying criteria, the judge will have to dismiss the case.

Finally, whenever the statute of limitations has expired, YOU should send an "Expired SoL Letter" that informs the collector of this and that you are aware of the expired SoL defense and, if the collector pursues court collection efforts, you will use it as your defense. Sending this letter stops most collection actions because collectors won't waste their time and resources on an expired debt when they know the debtor knows the debt has expired.

However, unless you inform the person trying to collect the debt that the statute of limitations has expired, or bring it up during a court appearance, the collector stands a good chance of winning a judgment against you.

Use the free sample letters on my site: **www.debt-n-credit-letters.com/**

Some Final Thoughts

My purpose in writing this book is to help as many people as possible deal with collectors and creditors who skirt the law and use illegal and unethical collection tactics.

I hope this guide has provided you with the tools and information necessary to Control the Ball! I plan to update and revise this book as often as necessary. However, keeping track of the many laws and rules at both the state and federal level is a daunting task, one where I could use some help.

If you know of some rule or law that you feel others should know about, please e-mail the information or a link to the information to me. Also, if you find any discrepancies in this book, I would appreciate an e-mail letting me know. I've gone to great lengths to ensure accuracy, but mistakes do happen.

I was once broke and homeless and worked many years to overcome the problems caused by my loss of financial stability. But I did it, so can you!

Although I've provided information and tools necessary for you to protect yourself, you need a solid mental attitude if you're to successfully thwart unethical collectors. You must convince yourself that you are a good person who has fallen on hard times. Hard times happen to the best of us.

Convincing yourself that, in spite of your situation, you are still a good person will help you regain your self esteem and it will help you stand up to debt collectors who try to bully you. Remember, no matter how deep in debt you are or how far behind you are in paying valid debts, you have rights. Control the Ball and you really can fight back!

I wish you the all the best…

Sincerely

Rich Rafferty
Rich's Enterprises, L.L.C.
Prattville, Alabama
http://www.debt-n-credit-letters.com

Visit my other FREE websites to help you deal with debt/credit issues…

http://www.creditcardsed.com/
http://www.debt-n-credit-letters.com/
http://www.student-loan-default.com/
http://www.filing-bankruptcy-form.com/
http://www.chapter-7-bankruptcy-forms.com/
http://www.chapter-13-bankruptcy.com/
http://www.child-support-collections.com/
http://www.debt-n-loan-consolidation.com/
http://www.fair-credit-reporting.com/
http://www.small-claims-courts.com/
http://www.stopping-banks-foreclosures.com/
http://www.personal-finance-loans.com/